Valley So Sweet

BOOKS BY BERT RAYNES

*Birds of Grand Teton National Park
And the Surrounding Area*

*Finding the Birds
of Jackson Hole*

Valley So Sweet

by
Bert Raynes

❧

Illustrations by
Rebecca Woods Bloom

White Willow Publishing
Jackson, Wyoming

First Edition, Printed October, 1995

ISBN 0-9642423-1-1

There is not in the wide world
a valley so sweet
as that vale in whose bosom
the bright waters meet
Oh! the last rays of feeling
and life must depart,
Ere the bloom of that valley
shall fade from my heart.

❦

Thomas Moore
1779-1852

FOR MEG RAYNES

And for everyone who appreciates the wonders of the natural world.

Acknowledgments

I know where to start making my sincere acknowledgments to all the good people (and animals and places) who have influenced me, who continue to educate and impress me. I begin with my wife, Meg Raynes. She's been at it for some time, and about has a handle on it.

Then, on to friends who not only influenced me but also gave valuable support and advice on this book: Louise Lasley, Becky Woods, Tim Sandlin, Rich Bloom, Mike Casey, Bronwyn Minton, Jan Hayse, Bruce Hayse, Mary Shouf, Mike Sellett, Connie Wieneke.

It gets tougher at this point. I don't know quite how to continue, for I wouldn't know how to stop. So much help and support in one's life, words of instruction and direction and caution, spoken words, written words, words not spoken. So many teachers, colleagues, collaborators, idols, fellow students. How to separate them, how to attempt to list them all? How to chance overlooking someone? How indeed, to thank wildlife for being wild, a beautiful sky for being beautiful? How to reward our pets?

With reluctance, and by your leave, friends, I settle for an all-encompassing and sincere thanks to you, and you, and especially, you.

Contents

❦

Introduction

❦

T he study of natural history has been one of the gifts
in my life, a serendipitous present I received after
most of my formal education — and a significant per-
centage of my formative years — were complete. I spent my
first 16 years in an urban setting within a family indifferent
to, and timid of, the outdoors. My chosen career as a chemi-
cal engineer brought me no closer to the world of nature.

Marriage saved me from missing the animals and trees,
the mountains and sunsets. By great good luck, I met Meg, a
small town girl who became my wife. Under her gentle tu-
telage, and with her encouragement, my awareness of nature and so much more gradually expanded. We started hiking, camping, and flyfishing. Then birds came into our life
and we became reasonably diligent bird watchers. Bird
watching led me into other aspects of natural history, into
myriad fascinating areas.

We've since birded and enjoyed the outdoors everywhere we've lived. Meg and I moved to Jackson Hole, Wyoming, almost a quarter of a century ago, and here we mean
to stay. In these years I've been thrice fortunate: I get to watch

nature, often up close; I get to watch nature mostly in the Rockies; and I get to write about natural history and other topics in a column in the Jackson Hole News, a weekly newspaper.

Writing was always an important part of my work in research and development. I like to write. I admire the English language. The opportunity to write a newspaper column was unexpected and is a challenge I enjoy. Some of the small essays in the book have their origins in that newspaper series. I try to describe events a constant observer — without specialized equipment and skills — can notice and appreciate.

While not abandoning this theme, the book is also a personal journal written over a number of years. I don't mean to give the impression I'm always alone. My best times have been shared with Meg, our puppies, and an odd assortment of characters: birdwatchers, historians, geologists, botanists, insect guys, biologists. Despite our lack of training in biological disciplines or wildlife, together we achieved a little comprehension of the natural world. We continue to work on it.

But, you know, gravity works all the time and life happens. Meg can no longer accompany me on some outings, and my own hikes have become short and slow. I don't like to inconvenience anyone who can still swing his or her legs without conscious thought or discomfort; it's a pain in the neck for them, and it's a pain all over for me. So I use the walk-the-dog ploy.

And I still write about this corner of the Rockies. We live in Jackson Hole because we choose to. It's a place of long, cold, snowy winters and relatively short, often cool, summers. Autumn starts early — by Labor Day it's apparent — and with great luck may extend more than a month or so. Spring is sometimes on a Tuesday.

The Hole is also a part of the country where it's not a great idea to run through town on the winter solstice and proclaim that spring is coming. Not a way to make friends. Too many people have just begun settling into winter: ranchers and farmers who depend upon snow for summer irrigation, recreation interests who look for snow to attract well-heeled persons to play on and in. Yet there is — or there is for me — satisfaction knowing the solstice has arrived, a new year has begun in the natural world, and that I'm looking for and sometimes find the signs.

I hope there's some satisfaction for you, too. Journey with me now on a stroll through a year in the Rockies. I start in December with the winter solstice. Come along whenever you can.

> Bert Raynes
> Jackson Hole, Wyoming
> 1995

Winter

A New Year

❧

I t's a couple of days past winter solstice. In another few days, the calendar will turn and it will be New Year's Day. The sun will set a few moments later this afternoon than yesterday. Although it hasn't yet begun to rise earlier, today the sun will send a few more photons to strike the earth. Nature's new year has already begun.

Truthfully, my heart doesn't accept what my head knows. I can read about the winter solstice. I can find and accept sunrise and sunset tables. But I can't prove it by me. Where is some evidence I can discern by myself? It isn't in my sense of lengthening daylight, nor is it in the temperature. It's cold today; in the Rocky Mountains the coldest winter temperatures occur from mid-December through February. Should it be storming, the day seems just a temporary brightening that too soon fades to black.

I am sobered by the realization that so many ancient peoples and societies determined solstices with accuracy, yet I have never bothered to make an independent observation. No minor Stonehenge, no Sun Dagger, no sunbeam disappearing into a hole in an adobe wall. I have a convenient foothill I could use to monitor where the sun rises and I could—but I don't—mark its passage at dawn; I have real mountains behind which the sun sets that I could use as a ruler, as my demarcation—but I don't do that, either. Perhaps I'm afraid I'm not smart enough.

As I walk through a scant foot of snow I wonder about the people who inhabited the Far North. How did they endure the days and months when the sun never rose? Where was there some assurance if they hung on a little longer—another couple of non-moons, non-sunrises, non-sunsets—light would indeed return? A non-sunrise can't be marked, even if one is smart enough to want to follow it.

Mountain Chickadee

They had faith—and I freely admit—far better powers to read subtle signs than I have. In that regard, modern celebrations centering around the winter solstice ignore or downplay the relief and joy once felt when some sign, some marker, pointed to return of the sun. Return to spring, to summer and easier times. Return of edible plants and animals and birds. Return to life itself.

On this December day my faith in what I've read about the solstice is being tested. My immediate world seems featureless, flat, silent. Evergreen trees reveal nothing. Deciduous trees and shrubs appear lifeless, stark. Have roots and buds, hibernating animals and insects in their eggs truly reacted to the solstice? Has a root stirred, a bud enlarged? I can't tell. The sky offers no clues. What I see ahead doesn't seem any different from where I am, from where I began my walk.

Then, suddenly! A band of two—no, three—chickadees materializes and occupies a small aspen grove close by. One, a mountain chickadee, chatters then falls quiet before delivering a two-note song, a *peah-wee*. That song, that spring song—tentative, as yet unpracticed and half-whispered—is my sign, the evidence I seek.

That tiny chickadee recognizes the season has turned, although I cannot tell it. Perhaps I know better than this little bird how long it is before winter loosens its grip upon the land and all creatures. Perhaps not. But that chickadee is already certain it will happen. I feel better about everything; a little bird has given me my first clue, the impetus to look for more. And since I'm one of those anthropomorphic types, I speak right up to these little birds, and say, "Thanks. Thanks a lot. Hope we all make it."

When It's Really Cold

On New Year's Eve, 1978, the temperature plummeted to 63 degrees below zero. The big ugly powerline—a hotly debated monstrosity that destroyed the view but promised an end to power failures—contracted sufficiently to sever.

Blackness was immediate. A cold hand on house, hearth and flesh fell almost as quickly. We instantly knew this cold was different from others we'd endured: It was one of those times thought of one's survival sufficiently concentrated the mind.

If you haven't yet gone through such a sequence—and the relative values would be different if you live in a hot desert or mild semi-tropical place—I'll tell you that zero degrees is one cold, minus 10 another, minus 20 different still. All are tolerable. Minus 30 is a lot colder, minus 40 is damn cold. Minus 50 is unbearable. Lemme tell you, minus 60 is hell headed north.

Automobile bumpers can, and do, fall off when bolts

crystallize and fracture. Plate glass windows shatter. Trees snap as sap freezes, expands and explodes plant tissues. Water pipes, even water mains, freeze up. Sewer lines freeze: Imagine the fun.

Horses and cows stand still. Stock still. No pun intended.

The house gets colder. No power. Only one inefficient fireplace, one stove. No water. Almost time to drain the pipes. If it goes on longer it will be time to go elsewhere – if the car will start.

At minus 60, combustion engines don't want to start, transmissions don't want to turn, vehicles don't want to move. Tires are square. Well, flat on one side. Some people start fires under their cars, using charcoal or logs to thaw gas lines. Some people don't burn their cars up doing that sort of thing. I'd never try it ... I don't think.

People whose cars start don't turn them off until it warms up, so smog and fog build up. Buildings that still have heat steam, creating yet more fog.

After a couple of very long, very frigid days (and half a cord of firewood) the power came back on. The cold snap thawed, zooming up to minus 35. But! It thereafter never got above minus 35 for three long weeks. It was those weeks – weeks of unrelenting minus 35 days and nights – that got to my psyche. No wind, thankfully, and glorious sunshine, spectacular days ... but long after the weather returned to seasonably above zero days and modestly cold nights, I believed it to be minus 35. I dressed for minus 35, thought it was minus 35, planned my day for minus 35. Had I not recognized this psychological hang up, and fought it aggressively, I don't know how many winters it may have persisted. It was not easy to get over 63 degrees below zero.

I don't care to experience that kind of cold again. My psyche might not be able to handle it twice.

Dipper Delight
❦

The calendar says it's a new year. The Intermountain Region has been locked under a high pressure weather pattern—a regime as it is sometimes called. Cold days, colder nights. Little wind. Sunshine delayed until lingering morning fog burns off. No precipitation.

Ponds and creeks have frozen solid. Elk and deer wander across the ice, leaving both recognizable paths and random patterns. The river is open, ice floes and clusters of crystals whispering down. Year-round, the river runs fast, runs powerfully. It is the Snake, running still clear and not yet fully tamed where I live.

The river runs so fast most wild animals are content not

to challenge it, seeking its edges whenever possible. A few creatures delight in the challenge, none more than one bird: the dipper, or water ouzel. I say "delight" deliberately, for I have no difficulty accepting animals as well as mankind permit themselves identical emotions: play, chagrin, apprehension, a sense of well-being. Call it blatant humanization if you must; I call it insight based upon observation.

Dippers, otters, waterfowl, and humans delight in river play. In January, in the Rockies, at 25 degrees below zero, you can almost forget about humans.

I spend a little while, in my delight on this minus 25 degree morning, watching a dipper carefully yet enthusiastically work an overhang.

Here, the river has lapped at snow to create an ice shelf. The dipper is singing at work, walking with nonchalance in and out of the water, hopping indifferently on exposed cobbles, snatching aquatic insects, and bouncing. Dippers bounce above water. (Underwater they "fly" or walk, but I don't think they bounce.)

With each bounce a white membrane, the third eyelid, flashes over the eye--semaphoring some message, some private joke perhaps. Probably not. There must be a reason for the eye flash, and I suppose I ought to try to find out sometime. Maybe when it's warmer.

Meanwhile, I stand in my tracks, watching the cold, bracing morning, taking delight in the spirit and verve, the dashing and notes and song, of the dipper. On this morning, New Year's Day, no other bird or animal — other than our puppy — is seen or heard. No duck, no raven, no chickadee, no deer, nor coyote. There's sign of porcupine and moose, and dog (including ours); but only sign. I hear my breath, my step, the water — and the sleek little dipper. One last trill and it flies off on stubby gray wings. I'm alone once more.

Trolls, Fairies And Leprechauns
❦

Ugh. An ugly morning.

No way around it: Ugly. It's not all that cold for January; minus 8, almost balmy. But at 8:00 a.m., a good 30 or 40 minutes after the sun should have been up, it's still dark. Opaque. Impenetrable. Black.

I hope and trust that when this miasma lifts — today with luck — I can see the forest as well as the occasional tree. It's a rare time of year when the trunks of aspens are defined as dark against their background. Now, only trees and shrubs within a few feet can be detected.

Too bad. Each is strikingly beautiful; every branch, twig, and secret bud covered with delicate frost. White outlines drawn on a gray screen.

A unique combination of temperatures, humidities, rates

of cooling, an absence of winds and, I like to believe, a merry band of trolls, fairies and leprechauns, produces this delicate hoar-frost. It's an enchanted, ephemeral time. It might last an entire day and the next night, but that's rare. A breeze, sunshine breaking through, a rise in temperature, forces often too subtle for human sense to perceive – gravity, for all I know – almost always reduce the frost cover by mid-day.

The frost falls off bit by bit. Watch a particular tree and soon you come to think you're watching one of those time-lapse sequences. First a single flake, then a clump, later a simultaneous shedding.

A solitary raven passes through a lightening sky flying with some unknown purpose. Oh, heck, the purpose is to find something to eat.

The magic of the day subsides.

What? Magic? I thought it was an ugly day ... but that was earlier. Now, a person has to root for the sun over fairy dust. To root for the sun to dissipate the fog and do away with the frost cover. It is, after all, the depth of winter.

Ye must gather sunshine while ye may...

Raven's Portrait
❦

Some winter days I notice only a couple of bird species – if that many. Overcast windy days, all-day snowy days, days with no snow and no hint of sun. Grim days. Days when the full impact of a winter has to be acknowledged. Days when nothing stirs unless it must. Nothing except a raven.

A raven will not only be out, but likely riding the wind in seeming delight, playing the currents, chuckling to itself, searching the landscape for a bit of food. Some ravens migrate — or at least move down out of the mountains to less rigorous climates — but most stay put in their home territory. They shift around, moving to food sources. Since ravens aren't picky eaters, winter finds them near ranching operations, where big game animals congregate, around land fills, hard by potential carrion — wherever small mammals or insects might be active. And not just small mammals: When you're out on a trek or cross-country venture, don't be surprised to find a couple of ravens looking covetously at a hunk of your sandwich. Try not to look as if you are

faltering, either. (Nothing personal, of course.)

Ravens aren't good to eat; thus, man can watch them objectively if he chooses. Or reverently. Abundant evidence has established that many cultures not only revered ravens, but also learned from them, acknowledging their abilities and intelligence. Some peoples of the Pacific Northwest believed ravens created the world, its animals, even Man, teaching him how to survive and live.

Whether or not other societies subscribed to those particular beliefs, most have been aware of, fascinated by, ravens, and watched them for clues to and information about their environment.

Ravens are smart. They and their relatives have the largest brain relative to body size of all bird families. Presumably, that's why they are so smart and can learn by watching. Which leads to the question: If they're so smart, why don't they simply fly out of winter?

Maybe they stay to show us how to survive. Ravens talk to us. They chortle, call, chatter, and pronounce the prospect of a full crop to be good. They display their exuberance in flight, and do they ever know how to romance. After winter solstice ravens appear more and more frequently in pairs, performing intricate aerial ballets, perched side-by-side preening each other, muttering soft endearments.

Lessons to take to heart.

Winter

January Thaw

❦

The January Thaw is a Rocky Mountain myth that sometimes comes true. In those years the thaw occurs, what you get depends on where you are. On the east slope of the Rockies, the fabled Chinooks appear—warming winds which sweep away snow and ice from underfoot. Chinooks create physical, intellectual and psychological hot flashes.

West of the Continental Divide, the January Thaw is a brief reprieve from a steady routine of below freezing nights and days — a chance for creeks to open up a little, for a slope to bare up enough to entice foraging deer or elk, for a householder to find his door steps or path. (Storeowners apparently depend upon the thaw to clear their sidewalks.)

In high mountain valleys, the thaw lasts only a day or two. Winds scour out stale air and bring a hint, a vestigial remembrance that oh, yes, water does indeed have a liquid form.

It's a quotable phenomenon. "The January Thaw is not unwelcome, but it's fairly squishy and inevitably fleeting." "The thaw opens winter's door a crack through which one can see the certainty of March and April." " The worst one can say about any January thaw is that it doesn't last."

I look forward to the January thaw and seriously miss

it when the phenomenon doesn't occur. On the intellectual level, I find this odd, for I enjoy winter. I think it must be physical or psychological—a few hours of relaxation, per- haps—or a chance of reorientation.

Today I call out: Bring on the Thaw!

Ice Fishing
❦

For a good many years we went ice fishing. Mostly on Jackson Lake, but now and then on some of the smaller lakes we could reach on foot, or skis, or snowshoes. (We, ah, es- chewed snowmobiles. We couldn't wrestle one out of any place it might get stuck.)

We always waited, too, until there was at least six inches of ice thickness. We wanted to be confident that we wouldn't have any adventures we couldn't walk away from When out on lake ice and a temperature change or change in lake water level causes the ice to crack with a BOOM, that crack in the ice is always right between your feet.

Always.

And when the water in your fishing hole undulates af- ter that boom, it's nice to know there's some space for it to expand into. Somehow reassuring.

We enjoyed the walk to the ice. I liked to punch holes in the ice; it was warming and I could see how thick the ice was before we went too far in the deal. I drilled at least two holes and Meg got started when the first hole was open. She opened her folding stool, took off her gloves! and hat! and began to fish. I usually stood. She caught fish. I usually didn't.

She didn't get cold. People who catch fish don't, for some reason, get cold. People who don't catch fish, do.

Nevertheless, we each enjoyed ice fishing. We often went with a gang of other devotees and made a day of it. We shared stories and jokes and lunches. We pretended we were happy when some other guy caught a fish and congratulated him on his skill. Actually, it was usually a her we had to congratulate. No, not Meg, who wasn't bad at this game, but another gal who always, I say always, outfished *everybody*. Simply everybody, every time. She'd catch fish when she paid attention, and when she didn't. She caught fish if she lit a cigarette or took a bite of sandwich or dropped her rod, or dozed off. She caught fish in her hole or in yours, if you got so exasperated you made her switch with you. She caught fish with your lure, your rod and you didn't with her gear.

It's a miracle she survived.

Of course, you're out there on flat ice with no cover, no place to hide or conceal anything. That helped her.

Oh, yeah. Out there in the open, when someone calls out, "Look at the mountains," it's only polite to look at the mountains for a decent time interval.

16

Winter

First Tracks
❦

Not so long ago as I like to think back on it, once in a great while I would make the first ski tracks down some trail. Most enjoyable, to be out when the only other sign was made by some wild creature.

It happened again the other day — to my astonishment — after a nice overnight dusting of snow. One of those snows which isn't predicted or expected, when the barometer seems stuck in place. Yet, come morning, there's this irresistible tabula rasa. It was fairly early when I started out and so I was indeed the first human there that day. Hilary was first puppy. The wild critters beat us both: There were already lots of tracks on that cold canvas.

I'm not a skilled tracker. I've studied and studied Olaus Murie's classic book on tracks, but tracks are, apparently, not my thing.

Oh, sure, I can tell deer tracks from elk, or snowshoe hare from porcupine, say. Coyote perhaps six out of ten times. River otter, muskrat, skunk. If I'm lucky.

I don't get bison dung confused with cattle or horse droppings.

I've mastered the more or less easy identifications. But I puzzle long over what might be weasel or marten, red squirrel, mouse or vole—and especially tracks which look to me as if a tiny precision stamping machine had gone mad. When I find tracks difficult to decipher (even as to proper family, for Pete's sake!) I'm sometimes relieved when our cocker spaniel snuffles out the evidence.

This personal mental block vaguely disturbs and vexes me, because there aren't *that* many animals whose paths I might cross in deep winter in the Rockies. A dozen and a half, tops; and I'd have to be exceptionally fortunate or on a long trek to come across five or six. On this day I think I recognize fresh moose tracks and sign, an old porcupine track, some mysterious prints scampering from one half-covered sagebrush to another, and long-tailed weasel tracks.

Myriad old tracks follow the river edge and snow-covered gravel bars, where geese and ravens occasionally gather. I've seen otter tracks and short slide paths in the past. Twice I've seen mink, in the flesh. The river proper is open and swift, but shallow portions are frozen; deer cross these areas indiscriminately.

I find where deer have lain and pawed through the snow for grasses and forbs. No big accomplishment on my part; here, my path is a roadway of hoof prints, pellets and yellow snow. I trudge off under the cottonwoods and spruce, the snow alternately bumpy, crusty, hollow and soft. Whichever critters have been traveling here have left no sign my eye discerns. I'd probably do better with snowshoes than skis; whenever I get bogged down on skis, I think I should have worn snowshoes. Blaming the equipment is another sign ...

Time to whistle up the puppy, circle back and pick up those strange uneven, too wide apart and hopelessly old-fashioned wide ski tracks. Some old fossil's tracks, looks like.

Let Go, Old Fellow
❧

We saw a bull elk die today. It was a bright cold day after a frigid night, after weeks of cold days and frigid nights; but it wasn't just the cold. And he wasn't simply old. He was a victim of sickness, or so worn out by the autumn rut he simply had exhausted his last resources. He could not — would not — focus on what was in front of him.

He was alone. Sick elk usually remove themselves from the herd. In fact, when you see a herd animal off by itself in winter, you should suspect it may not be healthy. Going off to die alone. A mechanism to protect the herd. Maybe just a little dignity in crisis.

This once splendid bull elk had gone off alone and been stopped by the National Elk Refuge fence. The refuge fence is a particularly tall, strong barrier intended to contain big animals; this elk could have been restrained by almost any obstacle. He stood, swaying with the effort to stand, barely breathing. It became obvious he didn't see, didn't smell, couldn't react to the dozen or so once dreaded humans who crowded in front of him, a wire's width away, taking pictures. They offered grasses for him to eat, reacting as to a zoo animal or to a cute, domesticated horse.

They simply didn't recognize what their eyes were registering. They didn't understand what was happening a few feet away.

There was no known physiological reason for the elk not to be able to see—he probably lacked energy to react. There was no known physiological reason the people couldn't understand what was occurring.

A young boy did. "Let him alone," he hollered. "Don't you see he's dying?" The startled crowd dispersed. One person was angry, most were abashed. Most, finally comprehending.

By then the bull was down, head back as though he was running wild and free through the lodgepole forest, still young, still virile, eager to take on any challenge. And we whispered, "Let go. Let go, old fellow. Let it go."

Winter Sun
❦

Early this morning a great, full moon hung in a dark gray sky over Teton Pass, illuminating the landscape. Snow fields on the mountain tops glistened white; evergreen forests were not dark green but black. Patches of aspens were an indefinable neutral gray.

This moon has many names: Moon of Cold Coyote Noses or Moon of Holy Geez It's Cold. Something like that. It plowed its slow way through a clear sky last night—one of those near black-body skies seen in few places in the world, a sky in which the Milky Way defines the edge of light and black. It was one of those mid-winter nights on which if you paused and were still and looked up, you could feel, literally feel, the near-absolute zero of outer space, touch its immensity. The enormity of the universe and the insignificance of your own self.

And you better be wearing a hat with ear flaps.

This morning, at daybreak, it's cold. Even colder than at 3 a.m.. Cold but with a promise of a pleasant sunny day. The sun will be good to see. One doesn't have to be a SAD sufferer to feel energized by winter sun — or a misanthrope to get growly at friends and family after a week of featureless gray days.

The sun is the engine driving this planet and our psyches.

At just this moment, this moment between night and day, it's quiet. It's a waiting ... not an ominous quiet, a pause. Night creatures have found places to rest. Day creatures are just stirring, not yet on their various pursuits.

A raven beats his way across the sky. Soon another leaves its roost to commence the daily business of keeping alive. The sky has lightened and now has a suggestion of blue.

I'm scuffling along the river bank. A dipper forages in the riffles he has adopted this February. A pair of goldeneyes swims slowly away from me and the puppy; I notice the hen's bill yellowing and the male is distinctly a Barrow's golden-eye. Ahead, a long way down river, is the slightly hulking, massive silhouette of a bald eagle, circling near last year's nest site. A coyote calls briefly ... a location call? Moose and elk tracks, but no animals I can see.

I'm glad there's no wind. I'm thankful for the warmth of the sun's rays. The big engine of our little solar system is getting cranked up. Makes me glad. Makes me grateful.

Wanton Destruction
ᵂ

Cold again last night. A nearly cloudless sky. Winter constellations glittering away. I know people who name arrangements they claim to recognize in night skies. These are otherwise reliable types, so ... I suppose.

The cold night litters the landscape with diamonds in the snow — crystals perched at every conceivable angle, covering every solid surface, each reflecting and refracting the slanting rays of the rising sun. Prisms, mirrors, sparkles of ice hanging on trees and shrubs, clinging to the few tufts of grasses not covered by snow. On tree branches and needles. Everywhere.

It's beautiful. And crunchy. Every step smashes dozens upon dozens of these wondrous creations, these ephemeral aggregates of frozen water molecules. Pity to destroy them all. Puts me in mind of trampling wildflowers in some alpine meadow in July. Simply can't avoid their destruction. Thousands, billions, disappearing as I wander without purpose except to mess up the synthesis of proper temperature, humidity, rates of cooling, absence of wind and molecular layer-by-layer atomic growth.

What a swell way to start a day!

My Mountains

On this February morning the southeastern horizon lit up with a luminous peach and yellow glow. A couple of minutes later the mountains to my west and north were touched with rosy pink, a more common illumination.

There must be a simple explanation for this alteration of hue between east and west. I ought to be able to figure it out, and I will think more about it sometime. But right now, I simply watch the mountain peaks light up, the fading moon become the last reminder of the night, the day get underway.

When I referred to "the mountains," I could have said "my" mountains. They are the Teton Range, to my north and west. The Gros Ventres are east, the Snake River Range

Winter

The Grand Tetons

south and west. I'm in a "hole" ringed by peaks: Jackson Hole, Wyoming.

The Tetons have been so well described by so many I hesitate to add to the literature. But the Tetons won't mind, and besides, everyone sees them differently. The mountaineer judges them and names the possibilities; the geologist sees them before they rose and how they ultimately will become; the painter sees purple in them, a purple I have seen once in four decades; the romantic, the traveler, the skier, the pilot—everyone sees them differently. Even indifferently; we have met people whose casual glance at the mountains evoked no reaction whatsoever. Honest.

To me, my mountains appear different almost every time I look at them or think about them. Sometimes they fill the sky. Sometimes they look flat. Sometimes small. Today they look modest, and very cold. Even blushed with a robust pink-rose, they look pretty darn austere, remote, icy.

The sky is rather empty of clouds this morning, and as I move along, I recognize that it's empty of everything else. No sound. No bird. Makes me feel small ... maybe the mountains feel that way this morning, too?

Nah.

Mid- February days are short; there's no time to waste on lingering dawns. Fifteen minutes later — 20 at most — and I can't remember details of this one. Still no animal, no bird. The puppy doesn't need a second call to turn back. The prospect of a biscuit and a cozy corner appeals to her. Another cup of coffee sounds good to me.

Mutual Surveillance
❦

When this February morning's light snowfall stopped — an orographic phenomenon this time, not a "real" snow — the sun emerged fuzzily. We decided to drive up-country to look for sage grouse tracks. Probably too early in the year, we thought, but this particular winter the snow cover has been so light one can be seduced into thinking ahead to an early spring.

Driving past the National Elk Refuge, we note elk scattered throughout the big open flat at its south end, and judging by extensive trails, up into the surrounding low elevation forest. The refuge exists to provide supplemental feed to wintering elk when the animals exhaust available forage or the snow is too deep for them to reach it. They look to be in good condition. Three elk skeletons are visible from the highway, made easier to spot by scavenging ravens and coyotes. One carcass is host to two ravens and a coyote simultaneously. Odd. It's uncommon for ravens not to give coyotes more space.

All in all we see eight coyotes. Two pairs it appears; it's mating time for coyotes. The other four don't seem to be bonded, perhaps because they're prowling for voles and mice. Healthy elk pay little overt heed to single coyotes; but a constant mutual surveillance goes on. Indifference doesn't pay off in the wild.

A pair of bald eagles—two birds which look sociable together, in any case—watches the activity from a tall, leafless cottonwood tree. They may be subsisting largely on elk carcasses we can't discern. An estimated 7,000 elk winter on and around the refuge. Mortality averages around two percent, so the eagles watch and wait. Some winters a few roughlegged hawks winter on the refuge; not this year.

No sage grouse tracks could we find. However, we did see two moose and fresh badger diggings. Each mound of dirt erupting out of the snow had two sets of tracks going to and from it: badger and coyote. Little escapes a coyote's notice.

Mid-February and already aspen buds are noticeably swollen — enough that their clones are harder to peer into, enough that the fullness softens their silhouettes against the snow or sky. Enough that ruffed grouse have begun to utilize the buds for sustenance.

By late afternoon a chilly north wind has died. The sky has cleared of imperfectly formed lenticular clouds, and the Tetons look cold and stark. Relief comes as the mountain peaks take on an alpenglow. Quiet settles on the land.

The last of the alpenglow is extinguished. The Tetons look gray, even colder. We listen for coyotes, for any wild thing. Nothing.

We head for home and hearth.

Signals

Not yet two months past the winter solstice. The depth of winter. And yet the signals of spring are already here, if one looks. Sometimes it takes a hard look. Sometimes not.

Days are longer ... an odd familiar expression that means

daylight hours are lengthening; too often, nights are short-changed even in my journals. Coyotes are more vocal; their mating time isn't far off. On pleasant days, pairs of ravens sit together on a favorite perch, holding private conversations. On blustery, windy days, they soar in exuberant flight or perform aerial ballets with other paired ravens. Great horned owls call to each other in the night; they will mate and nest in the next few weeks. Chickadees forage in little flocks that appear loose but are actually small hierarchies. Now and again one or more will give a full-fledged spring song. Pleasant to hear, for there's promise in it.

A mid-winter afternoon sun reflects a welcome, delicious yellowish hue as it strikes willow stands, shrubs and trees. The shapes of a few aspens are so subtly altered that it might be your imagination; and yet there really is a tumescence of bud, a thickening of twig.

Signals.

For an unequivocal sign, look closely at the bill of a goldeneye hen being attended by a now overly deferential drake. It is already yellowing. Goldeneyes know spring is on its way.

Now, another signal as the afternoon begins to wane: mare's tails, cirrus clouds that herald weather change. There will soon be wind, and snow. This day one could imagine spring, feel it in his body and soul. By tomorrow winter will be back. No birds with energy to spare in play or song. The willows will be gray. Gray jays, already on the nest, sit tight. It will be difficult to remember spring tomorrow.

Bottoms Up
❦

A rather extraordinary winter phenomenon is commonplace in my part of the Rockies. Creeks, even sections of rivers, freeze not only on the surface, but from the bottom up! Since water ice is demonstrably less dense than liquid water and therefore floats (a unique and improbable property that enables Planet Earth to support life), it's counterproductive to see this bottom-up freezing in action. And a person has to see it himself to believe it.

I've just seen it, this February day. This cold day of cold days and nights. It perplexes me each time I witness it. At one time I believed what was happening was a freezing up of a stream section, forcing water flow to go up and over the ice jam ... with continued freezing at the air-surface interface. From the first ice jam up, and on and on. I was wrong. It freezes from the bottom.

This bottom-up hasn't happened, in my time of observation at any rate, unless there's been sub-zero temperatures for consecutive days and light snow cover. Without an insulating blanket of snow, the ground gets deeply cold and freezes the stream bottom. Anyway, that's what I think happens. My witness is certainly not unique; many Jackson Hole old-timers know that this does indeed happen.

Oh, sure, this is the 90s. Like everything else, there's mild controversy about the exact mechanism of this phenomenon. An alternative explanation postulates that when ice in a stream bed becomes sufficiently thick — in relation to the stream's flow rate and depth — the pressure of the ice forces the flowing water underneath it to break through and — yup — overflow the ice.

I've researched all the different theories: Each one is probably operative at one time or another. Or in concert. The result is what interests me more.

When this ice-up happens, streams eventually overflow their banks and flood their flood plains ... which in turn become ice bound. It's pretty to look at, but sinister. Hibernating or ground nesting creatures suffocate: Snow cover permits air to permeate whereas ice doesn't. Icebound shrubs and trees survive; they're dormant and don't require much gaseous exchange. Come spring, perennial vegetation grows and flowers and prospers, too.

Not so the animals. Prey/predator spring relationships are affected until rodents, amphibians, even aquatic insects rebuild their populations.

I recall one winter when a sudden thaw followed by heavy rain saturated the snow cover. A subsequent hard freeze turned the lower elevations and valley floor into impervious ice. The next spring and summer — and many summers thereafter — there were distinctly reduced rodent populations. Fewer mice, voles, ground squirrels, shrews and gophers correspond directly to fewer hawks, coyotes, foxes, owls, badgers, and weasels. It was a dramatic and memorable event.

The flooding I watch today is just as dramatic for animals and people in affected homes, but it's a limited scale event. I climb a few feet and estimate 35 or 40 acres are flooded and frozen over. The rest of the stream's flood plain is simply deep in winter, locked in protective snow cover. A widespread kill-off of small ground-dependent animals is probably not occurring, at least not from flooding and icing. Of course, animals can freeze to death, even while hibernating, should frost go deep enough for long enough. The expression "blanket of snow" is both poetic and accurate: The ultimate security blanket.

Suddenly, I'm cold. It's a fascinating topic and all that, but it's time to move about a bit and keep my circulation going. Don't want to ice up.

That Certain Day
❦

Meg and I've come first to recognize, then to anticipate, and now I think, almost to depend upon, a certain day in

February. It's that special day during which, for at least a few hours, we're certain spring is on its way. It's a juxtaposition of sun, temperature, and some indefinable ambience which sings to us: Spring. Kiddingly (I think) Meg says it's the day — usually in the afternoon while driving along on a particular stretch of highway with the car window open — that the beating sun melts the wax in her (left) ear.

Well, that's certainly specific enough. Were I still geared up to perform experiments, I'd attempt to determine the melting point or zone of her left ear wax ... at least I know now why she likes to have air conditioning in her vehicle.

Of course, we're not deceived by the sensation. We acknowledge the clear sky through which this wax-melting sunshine is streaming means in just hours or minutes, temperatures (and our ardor) will cool. By nightfall it will be again winter; by the wee hours, temperatures will be around zero or below. It is, after all, just February and months of difficult winter lie ahead.

Sometimes our February day comes in March. We've never felt it in January, though we've tried to believe it to no avail.

This year we stood in brilliant sunshine on a day in the first week of February. A stream gurgled cheerfully at our feet. For a few moments we watched a kingfisher as he sat studying it. The puppy snuffed snow softened by sun and proximity to the creek. The Gros Ventre Mountains rose to the east, the Tetons to the west. We asked each other if this was The Day. We wanted it to be, you see. Ah, but the clouds above the Tetons followed north-south prominences, clouds formed by high altitude, high velocity winds. Neo-lenticular clouds. And this wind was cold.

Try as we might we couldn't convince ourselves we'd feel so chilly on Our Day. I just *knew* that Meg's ear wax was, ah, unmoved. My ears, wax and all, were cold. Got to have each variable in place for a day to be designated properly. This was just another great winter day.

Maybe soon.

Melt Down

When spring approaches my tiny corner of the Rockies, snowfields reflect the sun a certain way — a glinting, a sheeting look, a glaze. Their surface warms and softens then refreezes in late afternoon to a mirror-like veneer.

Underneath, the snow recrystallizes, reshapes, becomes porous. Snow levels seem simply to diminish, decreasing in depth without too much distortion. A uniform reduction. Hereabouts, even a big snowfall doesn't alter the appearance of the terrain much. The familiar hills and canyons and mountains and flats look the same. Seldom, rarely indeed, does drifting snow obliterate a familiar landscape.

After the storm it's still what you expect to see, only freshly white and up a foot or so.

It works the same way during a melt. The snow goes away in its own good time and what was underneath emerges, but you knew what it would look like all the time anyway, so it's no surprise and it's all OK.

In the morning, it's possible even for a heavy-footed guy to walk on snow without falling through or having to slog. Can go almost everywhere the puppy goes. Puppy leaves almost no tracks. I do, but a minimum trail at that.

By midday, it's a wet world. The snow doesn't keep a little dog up, let alone me. Water trickles, seeps, pools, makes mud, makes puddles.

By dusk, the solid state of water prevails once more. It's March.

Snow
🍎

There are increasingly fewer days I think I can cross-country ski. Infrequent days on which the snow welcomes me, supports me, helps me go anywhere I choose. (I don't choose steep or even moderately steep slopes.)

I'm talking about skiing as a mode of getting around on snow, not as recreation or exercise. I use shoeshoes, too, for practical reasons. To get from one place to another, or to get off the beaten path. Strictly functional, sure; but I was having fun on this day.

Heck. For a couple of hundred yards I was Bill Koch with an 85-pound pack and one ski tied behind his back at an awkward angle.

Sometime in March, the snow pack metamorphoses. It reflects the sun differently, betokening a crust and forecasting the coming of spring. And making it easier for a shuffler to pretend he can move about effortlessly on his skis.

Snow exhibits many different characteristics. It's often remarked that Eskimos have separate words to describe snow — I forget whether it's 65 different snows or somewhat fewer. Anyway, a lot. Whatever its characteristics, it ALL blows if the wind picks up. Dry snow blows, wet snow blows, packed snow, old snow, new snow, pink snow, refrozen snow. It can all, somehow, blow.

Winter Rain
❦

It rained last night.

Not unpleasant to walk in to our car after our regular Wednesday evening of good talk, good food, and group acrostics puzzle solving. It was, however, about all the windshield wipers could do to keep up with it, and that's a hard rain in these parts. Had it been snow, it would've been a blizzard. It was snow higher in the mountains and on the passes.

Yesterday, ahead of this March storm, pioneering waves of robins arrived. A few solitary robins had been seen here and there for about two weeks. Most of the ground remains covered by snow, but there's enough bare ground harboring insects or earthworms, and a few shrubs with remaining fruits and berries to sustain a handful of robins. One has only to look along stream edges, against outbuildings, and by roadway edges for patches of welcoming earth.

This rain will be good for robins, for it will expose more soil. It'll be hell on other animals, though. A rain like this thoroughly wets down deer, elk, moose and other creatures who can't seek shelter. Cattle, too. This is about the time calves begin to drop around here. Sometimes I think ranchers just enjoy the challenge.

At the end of a long winter, energy levels and available food sources for wild animals run low. If temperatures plummet tonight or tomorrow, some animals will die. It's nature's way, but I don't relish the prospect.

Fog this morning. It was expected, since most of the ground remains snow-covered and the air is saturated. Relative humidity at 7 a.m. was a reported 97 percent; since I can't see even 100 yards, I say it's 100 percent.

Winter

Last night's rain is over. For now. People rhapsodize over snow and all its forms. And, oh, yes, they speak of gentle rains, nourishing rains, soaking rains, driving rains, devastating rains, and the one named after me, heavy Raynes. (Shoulda been gentle Raynes). Spring rains and chilling rains. Almost April. Winter began in October. I'm rooting for spring rain and the robins.

Mardy
❦

One of the great ladies and personalities America has yet produced, Margaret E. Murie, lives in Jackson Hole. We're lucky to know and love her. Mardy Murie has invested most of her 90 plus years as a champion of conservation and preservation in America and many other countries. She still does.

Mardy's late husband, Olaus, and his brother, Adolph Murie, were pioneer field biologists and writers who conducted studies of wolves, grizzly bears, elk, caribou and other species that set the standard by which modern field work is still judged. Mardy's sister, Louise, married Adolph; each lady made unstinting and non-grudging contributions to their husband's careers.

Mardy and Olaus always extended their friendship and affection, their separate and combined wisdom. They touched generations of people with similar and sometimes contrary views around the world. Mardy still touches them. The guest register at her home records names of presidents, cabinet officials, popular recording stars, famous authors, renowned scientists, unknowns, students, and lots of youngsters. I'll bet not many leave without having been influenced, charmed and educated. We certainly don't.

We visit Mardy at her home every Wednesday evening for acrostic puzzle night. One of Mardy's lesser accomplishments, but important to a fortunate few, is presiding over these weekly get-togethers at her comfortable cabin. They begin with guests sipping sparkling apple cider as they participate in an hour or so of genteel conversation: talk of books new and old, friends, local happenings. This is followed by a superb potluck meal and the even-paced solution of a puzzle undertaken and, invariably, won.

Acrostics are convoluted crossword puzzles whose unraveling normally requires consulting various reference volumes in Mardy's extensive libarary, in addition to the impressive intellects and memories of the half dozen to 15 or so friends and acquaintences in attendance. Mostly I take up space, and have been known to yield to the ambience and seduction of a wood fire.

These precious, low-key evenings have become our weekly renewal of sanity and grace.

Because of Mardy's warm hospitality.

Spring State of Mind

Spring is partly a state of mind. From one window of our home, the window next to our everything table, I see an almost solid expanse of snow. The deciduous trees are bare, although I want to believe their buds have begun to respond to increased daylight hours. Sagebrush pokes through the snow on south-facing slopes — gray, lifeless looking shrubs.

If I change my perspective by walking right up to the window, however, I can see bare ground against the south wall of the house. This isn't a result of heat loss through the house walls; it's from the sun's warmth, subliming the snow into the dry air. My spring is a little patch of bare dry ground that will one day be colored with tulips and columbine. It's less than 60 square feet, but I make a lot out of it: I'm of a mind to find spring today.

It's mid-March, a sunny day, with a slight breeze from the southwest. Although it's only 25 degrees, the snow on south-facing roofs is melting. The drips form icicles, which in their turn, drip. Insects appear. The house buzzes with mysterious, unidentifiable, unknowable flies...houseflies? Outside, creatures conveniently named snow flies and snow worms, as well as bugs and strange beetles, appear.

Winter

In a few weeks, days will arrive when a person can almost believe spring will return, a belief like a second marriage: triumph of curiosity over experience. On such a day a butterfly will flutter by, newly emerged from dormancy. A mountain bluebird will look it over in some pre-programmed anticipation, but return to hawking flies. I suppose these early butterflies don't taste good to a bird. Fortunately, I've never caught one to conduct my own experiment in curiosity. The truth is, I've never tried to catch one. I figure it tastes like industrial-strength antifreeze. This butterfly has been able to withstand extreme temperatures of 30 or 40 degrees below zero, hatch, then blithely fly about on a balmy pre-spring day, looking for plants to feed upon.

These are days to revel in, days that permit the eye to linger on green aspen buds and golden willow glow, days on which to shed a winter coat, a winter's habit, to embrace the unexpected warmth. Days to look and listen for migrating birds. Days to discover if bull elk have dropped their antlers, to wonder how much snow is left in the high country.

Followed immediately by winter, by horizontal snow and winds that bite deep into flesh yearning for warmth. Back to long underwear and boots and icy vehicle windows. To hunched glowering figures fingering cups of coffee or tea, staring out at more dang snow.

Back to winter.

Spring

Spring!

What is so rare as a day in Jackson Hole when the spring equinox has just occurred, and it's just like spring outdoors? And being outdoors with nothing else to do, in Jackson Hole, on that day? This time around the sun, vernal equinox and circumstances on the ground are in sync. It really is spring.

Spring! And just barely April. Is it an April Fool's joke? No: In garden corners violets and pansies are in bloom. Sage buttercups and orogenia flower side by side in the wild. Individual leaves of grass have greened up; by tonight they will merge into lawn. Willows flaunt color in twig and branch. Disappearing snowbanks reveal forgotten items: a garden hose, the barbecue, a ski pole. Couple more spring days and I may find the snow shovel.

Yesterday, cartop racks sported skis and snowboards; today, bicycles and kayaks. I see people sunbathing, people wearing shorts. In March. Heck, I remember when nobody wore shorts in Jackson Hole — not even the pretty girls. Not even in summer. (Of course, the county didn't spray for mosquitoes back then...)

Ground squirrels are emerging from hibernation and sitting on top of the snow. Perfect targets, one might think, for red-tailed hawks. One would be correct, for red-tails have begun to return. Sandhill cranes, too; they've been heard calling and seen circling over the buttes.

Chipmunks scamper about. Juncoes, Cassin's finches, robins and male mountain bluebirds examine nest boxes or nesting sites. Flickers yammer in the aspens. Trumpeter swans fly from feeding areas to inspect nesting locations still closed by ice.

And, today, a single swallow. A tree swallow, I guess. Not sure. It flew by going flat out, headed due north up the Snake River. Spring has arrived..

Whoa! First day of April. Let's just say winter isn't over, but the end may be in sight. Tomorrow the skis may be back on the cars.

Tug-Of-War
❦

Vernal equinox occurred less than a week ago. It was, I'd bet, right on schedule. A casual glance around the valley suggests it's still winter: Snow covers most of the valley floor and the mountains are completely entombed in white. Yet, winter is fading to spring.

The sun had it right after all ... the little rascal.

Against the south side of our home, tulips are up — some as much as four inches, even though four feet away the snow is three feet deep. Lilac and aspen buds are pregnant with life. South-facing slopes are baring up on foothill and butte. Along roadways, snow-free berms are dressed in winter drear and salt, wantonly spread against all intellect.

Red-tail hawks returned a few weeks ago, as did male red-winged blackbirds. Male mountain bluebirds are back in force. A few killdeer. The bluebirds are mostly silent; killdeer mostly noisy. Owls are courting or already nesting. Raven pairs are inseparable.

Bull elk are dropping their antlers. Coyotes have mated and selected their dens. Creeks open up more and more, increasingly attractive to waterfowl, herons and snipe. Almost daily another sign of spring surfaces.

Ah, but winter doesn't give up readily: It never does in these parts. Frost can develop on any day of the year, frost hard enough to kill corn or beans or tomatoes. That is a small continuing regret to me, I must say. A snowfall in mid-June on the valley floor is de rigueur. We once got stuck in snow on a Father's Day, along a short, shaded stretch of dirt road — despite a competent four-wheel drive vehicle.

Tonight it will drop below freezing. I used to believe a

third of our nights fell to 19 degrees. Wasn't sure why it was so precise; now I don't think it's so consistent a low temperature. For 20 years, overnight lows have increased in Jackson Hole and snowfall totals have decreased.

Perhaps in a week, perhaps in two months, a Rocky Mountain spring will be unequivocally here. That will be nice. It was nice on this late March day.

Roaring April
❦

March went out like a lion. Which means, of course, that April roared in.

The wind blew all night long. I remember, with more than a little nostalgia, when a spring wind was unusual in our valley, particularly at night. No longer true.

An all-night wind is a bit unsettling, and seems out-of-place in a high altitude Rocky Mountain valley.

There was snow on this wind, and so this morning there are my familiar drifts. With unerring accuracy and relentless, humorless persistency, snow fills the walk from the house, hides the steps, and is heaped where the car must pass in order to reach the large dump of heavy snow thrown by the plow at the foot of the driveway. I have almost come to terms with the idea that I pay (directly, in my case) for the plow to seal me in so someone else can proceed with abandon on the road (that I also pay directly for). Almost, but not quite.

Our deciduous trees are outlined with snow, so I judge that the wind dropped as morning approached. It's calm now; another clue, Sherlock. I suppose it's our low humidity, but seldom do evergreens on the valley floor retain much snow. Those spectacular pictures of snow-laden evergreens are normally taken at much higher elevations. Once in a while it happens that snow clings to everything and it's, well, stunning.

At about 9 a.m., the sun breaks through a thin cloud layer and patches of blue sky appear to the south. A promise that April will be a lamb, perhaps by afternoon of this very day. Things are looking up. What's more, I didn't get stuck.

Go For It, Spring

Early or late, long or short in duration, spring is a nice time. It's usually short in the Rockies. Spring flowers hurl themselves out of the ground to bloom next to banks of snow. Corridors open in the snow pack, allowing elk, deer, moose, and bighorn sheep to search out new green growth or settle for old forage newly exposed. Migrant birds begin to return, or pass through to more northerly regions.

Overwintering resident birds make their own obser-
vances of the changing season.

The equinox arrived a couple of weeks ago. Daylight
comes early, sometimes astonishingly early. Calves have
dropped on the ranches, antlers have dropped on the elk
refuge. We stroll without any real destination; just to walk
on dirt. If not dirt, mud. Or on not-ice, not-snow, not-slush.

We saunter about looking among last years dead grasses
and dormant shrubs for greenery. For some active insect,
an overwintering moth perhaps. For proof this old earth
will bloom one more time.

We meander to the imperative call of flickers, to the *ook-
a-lee* accompaniment of an anxious male redwing blackbird.
The sky—an incredible, indescribable blue—wraps us in
warmth, caresses the ground, encourages spring.

Go for it, spring.

Unmistakable Signs
❧

The first week of April, if not every April, we eagerly
seek signs of spring. We cruise along roads that bare up
earliest, looking for wildflowers: orogenia, spring beauty,
sage buttercup, yellow fritillary, violets.

Spring

One of the perennial wonders of a high altitude Rocky Mountain spring, to me, is the ability — if not the overpowering urge and capability — of plants to grow and flower immediately next to a bank of snow. Chlorophyll photosynthesis seems to be in the same league as gravity: irresistible. In a regime of zero degree nights and abundant snow cover notwithstanding, grasses green up and grow, wildflowers bloom, tree buds enlarge, and willows are sap-filled and supple wherever a bare patch of earth is warmed by the increasingly strong and prolonged hours of spring sunlight.

All it takes is the sun slipping behind a cloud or my entering a tree's shadow to appreciate the force of spring sun. My switch from heat receptacle to heat radiator is immediate, sudden, and self-explanatory. Looking for wildflowers is a wonderful excuse to stay in the open.

Responding to the sun, to the increasing supply of photons, to lengthening days, male mountain bluebirds have returned, picking off insects that have also responded to bare ground and flowering plants. Tree swallows are anticipated; any day now some lucky observer will spot this harbinger of spring. Osprey are already sitting on nest trees; we welcome the sight of a long-billed curlew as it crosses an irrigation ditch.

But, it's just April. By mid-afternoon a bank of clouds obscures the sun and it's suddenly cold.

No doubt about it: Cold.

51

Spring

By the time we get to the post office, pick up a grocery item or two and get home, it'll be cocktail time.

There are advantages to retirement. It may not be all skittles and beer, but a chance to look for wildflowers and wildlife on a whim isn't one of the negatives.

Renewal
❦

April! Patches of green up all over, improbable green grass. In just a day, huge landscapes of snow vanish. The melt water must be going directly into the ground somewhere; watercourses aren't muddied up and don't seem to rise. Aspen catkins have appeared, willows radiate splendid gold color. The parade of wildflower bloom has begun.

The dawn bird chorus now includes flickers as well as robins. Swallows are back. Canada geese and trumpeter swan pairs are staying close to preselected or historic territories; some are already commencing their nesting activities. Osprey and bald eagle pairs are back in business where open water permits. Cinnamon teal, pintails, shovelers and coots have returned.

Butterflies emerge and go boldly forth. Elk eye the north and yearn to move out of the valley to higher ground.

I have enjoyed this April day. But it's very early in April. Already there are cirrus clouds sweeping across the sky. Ah, well. Today was swell.

Spring

The Eagle/Raven Tango
❧

Afternoon and the setting sun is against me.

Scanning the foreground, trying to identify waterfowl with the sun before me, is both difficult and a bit hazardous. One doesn't want to aim binoculars or a telescope into the sun, naturally. Mallards, Canada geese, pintails, green-winged teal, baldpate: pretty good.

Sometimes the unexpected shows up. Last week it was a solitary snow goose.

A flash of wings to my side, at the limit of my peripheral vision, a vision that has narrowed. (My ears seem to be doing something akin to that, drat it.) Big wings. Ah ha — a bald eagle, on the ground, protecting a kill. Almost immediately, a raven sails past and lands a dozen feet ahead. No more than five seconds later, another raven lands, to the eagle's rear.

The dance begins.

The ravens walk this way and that, to and fro, around and around.

The eagle stays in place, occasionally looking down at its feet, pretending there's no one around. Even shaking its plumage to settle it, preening a feather or two. And making no move to eat.

I think the victim is a duck, an injured bird among so many, spotted by the eagle. Then, a raven jabs at the eagle's tail feather and eagle hops a few steps. I see it's grasping something small enough to be in one foot. The choreography continues.

As I watch this predator/scavenger/I got it/but I want it tableau, I wonder how long this scene has been played. Countless times over millions upon millions of years. Astronomical numbers of times.

Some anthropologists, if not most, think man started out as a scavenger. And why not. Opportunism works ... and a person doesn't need binoculars to spot it.

Watching this particular drama, I get the strong impression that not only the ravens are surprised at how small the catch is: The eagle is also. It begins to preen in earnest. The ravens wander off on foot, then take flight.

I leave. By auto. To observe whatever next act.

Spring

Winter, The Sequel
❦

Last night on our return home after a rollicking evening of dinner, conversation and acrostics puzzle-solving in a cozy cabin before a warming fireplace, snow squalls came in waves. Big flakes, kind of attractive. So I wasn't surprised on this April morning to find everything white outside.

Four inches of April covered trees, roads, fences, auto-mobiles, bird feeders, ranchland and roofs. It was either really pretty, or one more damn winter wonderland scene, depending on one's morning mood. To me? Pretty.

Spring snowstorms are informative. Migrant birds often are forced to earth in storms.

Many forage along road edges, snow-free sooner than most places. Thousands of birds can be seen at the edge of pavement, pecking at weed seeds, gravel, insects, and salt. Too much salt. I continue to be astonished at the popularity of road salt—especially here where it gets so cold salt either doesn't work to melt snow or, when it does, creates a slush guaranteed to freeze come nightfall. And the damage to roads, bridges, fisheries, automobiles: Ah, old boy, you've fought this fight and always lost; get back to your journal.

Spring

Last night's snow reminded me spring is a tug-of-war.
Winter is so long, so-o-o very long here, it rules everything,
living or inanimate, year-round. We hung Christmas lights
on our deck to celebrate a six-inch snowfall one Father's Day.
We've tried to grow beans, only to have them freeze on July
nights. It can snow in the mountains any day of the year.
Ephemeral snowfalls, sure, but real snow with well below-
freezing temperatures.

I decided, of course, that this wet snow was too sticky
to remove with a snow-blower, and shallow enough to keep
out of my boots. I ignored it. Standing there — checking out
the boot top/snow interface — I heard flickers calling. A pair
of Canada geese flew by, honking loudly. A robin clucked
from its perch of bare ground next to the house then reluc-
tantly flew off. Evening grosbeak and Cassin's finches ate
together, not always amicably, at the feeder. The mountain
bluebirds of yesterday were gone. American goldfinch appeared; they're getting yellower by the day, but won't nest
until thistles bloom in August.

Canada geese that were foraging in fields flocked this
morning in open standing water. The osprey nest which
supported its newly-arrived owner yesterday was empty but
for snow. Teton Pass looked marvelous; if I still skied I'd
enjoy darn good snow there. The mountains looked great,
snow where snow ought to be, the way one expects them to
look in winter/spring.

Spring

Killdeer, starlings and robins all foraged a thin strip of cobble lining the Snake River. Interesting. Barrow's goldeneye and mallards kept in separate flocks. Deer tracks and what I took to be muskrat tracks graffitied the landscape.

On a willowed bar in the river, a cow and calf moose munched away.

The sun came out, bringing instant warmth to me and the puppy. To the snow, too, which balled up on her feet. Cocker's feet do that trick with great creativity. Nobody enjoys walking on tennis balls stuck to his soles ... well, nobody I know.

I picked her up and we headed back to breakfast.

Death Recognition

We're poking around one of the places we go early in spring to hunt for wildflowers.

It's hardly a secret place: Kelly Warm Springs is adjacent to a plowed road. People drive here to see green when winter begins to drag. (Some people commence coming here by Thanksgiving, but they simply have a masochistic tendency, I fear.) It's April 1, and we could be on a fool's search. We don't think so. Sharper eyes have already seen orogenia in bloom.

Orogenia are tiny plants with dozens of inconspicuous

whitish blossoms on a stalk less than an inch long. They're hardy and almost always the first to bloom; if not for those special characteristics, they'd be noticed only by botanists. If then.

We luck out, largely because we were told they're up. And then, even luckier, we come upon a few sage buttercup also in bloom.

Three bull buffalo saunter down to sample the green growth surrounding the warm spring. Bison, actually, but most call them buffalo. We watch with a mixture of admiration, curiosity and a certain uneasiness. Although we believe bison belong in Jackson Hole and their presence enriches and enlivens the scenery — that they simply belong — some people who control the fate of these creatures don't want them around.

There came a spring day in 1989 when wildlife manag-

ers from various state and federal agencies concluded some bison needed to be shot. By-and-large, "game management" boils down to killing or not killing. This was a population reduction operation. Piece of cake. The bison were still on the National Elk Refuge, still in large groups, and conveniently near roads.

And so some uniforms were assigned (or volunteered?) to shoot 16 bison. Selected animals of every age and both sexes were killed. But there was a surprise: It turned out bison demonstrate an awareness of death in their kind.

When a female was shot, the remaining animals became agitated, excitedly moving about, tails up. First cows, then bulls, approached the dead cow to snuff, and sometimes nudge her carcass. One professional, experienced, management guy even went so far as to say their manner was "one of respect." (Gee. If I'd said that, he would have admonished me for being anthropomorphic. He'd be right).

When a bull was killed the entire herd went into a frenzy. Surviving bulls hopped about "like rodeo animals," bucking, bellowing, tails up, for up to 10 minutes. During this activity, many of the bulls deliberately gored and hooked the carcass. One bull which didn't die instantly was not only subjected to this savaging, but had another bull stand on him.

Cows were excited by the felling of bulls, too, but generally didn't participate in exaggerated activity. A few came up to sniff and to snort, but not to rake or gore.

We weren't witness to the killings or this death recognition business. Some 80 million buffalo were wiped out on this continent by — if not always literate, at least self-expressive — whites. We've read their exceptionally flowery and descriptive accounts of that near extermination. Examined paintings and seen movies. Read journals of travelers and hunters. But we have no recollection of hearing about this particular bison behavior. The stories portray professional hunters coolly killing first the lead cow and then the others as they stood there. Until the gun barrels got too hot to hold. One wonders if those old journals were edited, or if it just wasn't convenient for the killers to recognize feeling in their victims.

The killing on the refuge continued a second day. The remaining bison exhibited identical recognition-of-death behavior, but what appeared to the observers to be at a lesser level of excitement. Learning by the bison? By the killers? If by the bison, it was only learning of a sort, for after a century these animals still didn't grasp that firearmed man is their mortal enemy.

The game managers obliged (or delighted) to carry out this task appeared outwardly calm, detached. Professional. Yet, there were glimpses of behavior akin to a gang of nine or 10-year-old boys nervously bolstering each others' guilty consciences after committing what is nowadays termed minor vandalism. A crime, that is. Ooof. Enough of such thoughts. It's spring. Flowers. Sagebrush above the snow pack. Bluebirds. Bison in sight and a chance to see moose. Recognition of life.

Time to Strut
❦

In spring, it gets fancy.

Take sage grouse. Sage grouse aren't monogamous and don't pretend to be. They're into a modified harem arrangement in which a group of females are associated with a few males yet particularly attracted to — or by — one. In the case of sage grouse it seems clear one male can't — or doesn't — satisfy all the demands placed upon him.

This seems to be the fate suffered by males of many animal species, up to and including the higher primates. Things are tough all over.

We went to watch the sage grouse strut this morning. Sage grouse gather just before dawn at historically selected places which look like nothing special ... except to sage grouse. We call them "leks," areas where animals assemble to display and conduct courtship or mating rituals. Leks vary in size; some barely accommodate six males, whereas others extend several acres and are visited by 30 males and perhaps 120 females.

Spring

Our participation is simple. We show up at about 5:30 a.m. and position ourselves to have the anticipated dawn light at our backs. The grouse have already made their way to the lek, but sometimes a few more slide in on set wings from a half-mile or more away.

Pre-dawn on an April morning in Jackson Hole is cold. Sometimes it's windy and snowing. The grouse don't seem to care; we're talking raw sex here, so weather isn't a concern.

Soon we heard a peculiar plopping sound. This is an exhalation made by male sage grouse as they inflate then rapidly deflate air sacs prominent on their chests. Accompanying this display, they parade-strut with their spectacular tail feathers held erect and spread apart.

As the sky brightened, we perceived them clearly: a couple of big fellows in the middle of a loose circle of smaller, younger males and a gaggle of drab females pretending indifference. (Of course, it's feigned. They know it. Everyone knows it.)

Professional ornithologists — who too often are stolid and unimaginative — say that while the bigger, most aggressive male grouse are strutting around, showing off, and battling each other, a few females slip off into the sage with lesser-endowed, callow youth. Oh, well. I've noticed something similar in bars and on ski slopes. Nothing new.

I can't write about sage grouse mating rituals without

recalling an old incident that still tickles us. The biggest lek in Jackson Hole, historically, is on sagebrush flat occupied now by a large airport. Old-timers would simply go to the airport to watch the grouse. The grouse and the onlookers would be gone well before any aircraft were aloft.

As years passed the airport got busier, and bigger, and when airplane hijackings became a real threat, security concerns were solved in part by limiting casual access. Which is to say, they put up a big fence. Sage grouse observations fell off to almost nothing.

Meg and I got the idea to revive strutting watches. We approached the Grand Teton National Park administration for help.

The airport lies within GTNP and there is a guarded cooperation between the two entities. With great reluctance—a stance we have encountered on, well, almost every occasion we've addressed bureaucrats—a park naturalist agreed to arrange a supervised visit to the airport lek. I won't mention his name, but I remember it. He bet us that no more than five people would attend, and if that was the case, we could forget bothering him ever again. About anything.

He underestimated the pent-up urges old-timers had to revisit that spectacle; the interest of a small bird club; and the power of a newspaper column alerting people to this opportunity.

Spring

So did we. As we drove to the airport (on what turned out to be a beautiful, calm morning) we were surprised at the volume of traffic passing us. Lots and lots of cars. We wondered where everyone was going at 5:15 a.m.. It wasn't hunting season. Way too early for skiers. Slowly it occurred to us: People were going to look at birds.

And, they were. There were almost 70 people that morning. Lots of fun.

Oh, yes. By the very next Sunday the park had assumed authority over sage grouse observations. Personnel showed up in uniform, with red flashlights and for all I know, guns. They had a fancy hand-out for each attendee on the natural history of sage grouse. No mention, naturally, of anybody outside the park service. Ha! (That naturalist, by the way, used the entire affair to enhance his resume and advance his career. He is stationed elsewhere now, probably where he doesn't have to get up so early.)

But, that incident wasn't on our minds this morning. We just watched the birds, enjoyed the sights and sounds, and trusted in another generation of sage grouse. As the sun crested Sleeping Indian Mountain, the grouse skipped away into the snowy sage flat. We believed we didn't influence the birds in their activity. Perhaps we even kept a coyote at a distance, but we don't know that for certain.

Time for breakfast. I'm not at all certain what grouse do après strut.

Rest, probably. Or smoke.

Spring

Birds Do It
🍏

It's a warm early spring day along the north end of Jackson Lake. The snow is melting but firm.

Snowshoes are working out pretty well. We're not going far, just to a vantage point to see if a particular bald eagle's nest is active. To see if anybody is home yet. We have a telescope, binoculars.

The nest appears to have snow in it, so we think ... but then Meg notices an adult eagle perched higher in the nest tree. All right! We watch it, scanning the lakefront trees for another eagle. Suddenly, Meg announces it's alert, looking skyward. We look up, but see nothing.

The eagle launches and begins to circle up, flapping heavily.

Directly overhead we hear the odd high-pitched, rapid chatter bald eagles sometimes make. It comes from a second eagle, high up. In a swoop, wings partly folded, it dives toward the nest and the ascending eagle.

A battle? A migrating intruder? A sub-adult bird that needs to be driven away? This time of year, in the northern Rockies, bald eagle territories are still to be established. Some eagles have long distances yet to go to summer hunting and nesting ground. Some of these migrants pass peacefully

65

Spring

by; others need a little direct urging from an established bird.

The distance between the eagles closes quickly: It's no battle. The swooping bird pulls up and begins to circle the other in ever-tightening circles, both rising on a thermal. The newcomer is the larger of the two.

Both birds call. The smaller extends its feet, coming closer. A few more circles and the larger eagle extends its feet. The smaller turns on its back and the pair clasps talons, tumbling toward the ice and snow-covered lake in an aerial crack-the-whip.

They separate, circle, climb, call: They court. This is unmistakable, let-it-all-hang-out, just-you-and-me-babe courtship. They grab each other again, this time falling further down, separating barely above the ice.

And then, it's over. One eagle flies back to the nest tree and perches. The other flies south, out of sight.

Too bad we quit smoking. Oh, well. We pack up and head back to the car, settling for hot coffee.

Dance of the Cranes
❦

It's 10 p.m.. We're camped, in style, in a national forest campground near Grays Lake National Wildlife Refuge, Idaho. It's cold—only 20 degrees—but we're in a truck camper equipped with a heater, toilet, range, stove and refrigerator — not to mention a really comfortable bed with two sleeping bags and a foam mattress.

I remember when we graduated to this thing. After years of tents and air mattresses on lumpy ground and sleeping bags soggy from rain, it took only one whole evening — and two gin-and-tonics with ice — to get us thoroughly accustomed to it.

We're at Grays Lake to witness sandhill crane courtship. To see them dance. We decide to take a short nap in anticipation of an early morning outing.

A great horned owl hoots somewhere pretty close. It's just like those movies and TV shows. Loud, deep, resonant...

It hoots, and hoots. We listen, and listen. Then, an answer. A deeper voice, far off. For 20 minutes the owls call back and forth, the husky-voiced paramour moving closer, until they seem to be calling from one location, in a sotto voce locution.

We fall asleep. At two o'clock, the owls are still chatting companionably.

The next morning we watch sandhill cranes dance. Theirs is an elaborate, highly ritualized courtship — and for good reason: Cranes pair for life. "Forever" relationships benefit from constant reinforcement. (Remember that, children.) Throughout the year sandhill crane pairs engage in unison calling. The birds stand either side by side or facing each other in a distinct erect posture, and make strident simultaneous utterances. This communication may last only a few seconds or go on for a minute or more.

In spring, unison calling is often followed by dancing. The dancing of cranes is extraordinary. (Some Native American tribes created wonderful dances based upon the rituals cranes and grouse perform.) These great long-legged birds lower their heads while lifting and spreading their wings. They then abruptly lift their heads and downstroke their wings, often jumping several feet or more into the air on this upward movement—a *jeté*. Sometimes they dance in synchronism, a feathered pas de deux. Other times a whole group gets into the spirit of things. Imagine the Radio City Rockettes *not* in a line.

Neither unison calling or dancing necessarily lead directly to copulation.

THAT follows a "parade-march" approach by the male to the female. He carries himself erect, from his tertial feathers, to his expanded crown, to his upward-pointed bill. Heaven knows what else is erected.

If the female is willing, she spreads her wings in semi-extension and lowers her body to a slanted posture. If she isn't willing, he has wasted all that parading.

And everything else.

By about high noon, both we and the cranes are tired of the entire business. They begin to feed.

We have lunch. So it goes.

Spring

Osprey
❦

This morning an osprey was perched on its nest, a home of sticks and mud balanced on a powerline pole overlooking the Snake River.

It's newly back, for it wasn't there yesterday.

I say it wasn't; I didn't see it is all I mean. I would venture to say "he" because this morning he demonstrated the extent of his territory to two bald eagles—one an adult, the other younger. Eagles nest a short distance down river, and the osprey wanted this pair to consider his boundaries.

It was serious stuff. The eagles chased the osprey until he gained elevation. Eagles outfly osprey when osprey are carrying fish. Unencumbered by a fish and eager to claim its territory, this osprey flat out-flew the eagles. It was aerial combat: serious, silent, skillful.

Eventually, the eagles separated, the fully adult bird flying downstream in a straight line. The younger eagle circled, staying well within sight of the osprey nest. Finally, the osprey got fed up and dove towards the younger eagle from great height. The eagle flipped twice on his back, talons extended, then flapped off to the northwest.

I guessed that this osprey is back and ready for courtship. I'd like to know what his testosterone level is ... probably equivalent to a doctor's, or a trial lawyer's, or a fighter pilot's.

A half hour later another osprey appears.

For several minutes, the two birds fly in slow circles centered over the nest, peaceably and in silence. I guess it's a female but not his mate of last year; after seven or eight minutes he returns to his nest and the newcomer flies up river.

During the winter I sometimes see a bald eagle sitting on this osprey nest—not to claim it, but to use as a fishing perch.

The nest overlooks a stretch of river inhabited by trout and whitefish. In summer, after territorial imperatives are worked out, eagle and osprey will each utilize this resource. Carefully. Watchfully. With some fish stealing by the eagles to be sure, yet with a certain respect for the nest site.

For now, the osprey sits and watches. And waits.

April Days
❦

A Sunday morning in April. Paschal full moon day, the day around which several religions elaborate their respective faith.

There was one shaft of sunlight early, lasting about a

minute or so. Then the fog settled in, followed by a splash of rain and snow. Yesterday was grand; today everything looks weary. Even the fresh aspen buds look tired. The river, gray. The rimed cobbles of the river bank look gray, too, although close inspection reveals every color of the spectrum. The mountains have disappeared.

The bird feeders are busy, very busy, but no bird sings. They hardly spar; eating is too important. Cow calves lie quietly and apparently safe, nestled close to their mothers; it's still warm, but it might yet get cold and life-threatening. It'd be nice to get reliable weather forecasts but that technology hasn't arrived in the Rocky Mountains. If anywhere, come to think of it. I size up the morning and dress and behave accordingly. Like a new calf, except calves don't have a clothing option.

Puppy urges that we go out on her walk, so we do. Once out she holds back, not anxious to get wet. It's quiet everywhere. Pairs of ravens fly over in silence. Robins forage quietly. Three Canada geese sail in, making short comments to each other about proposed landing sites. We proceed onward a short distance, the snowfall briefly increasing in intensity. And then, a flash of fire as a red-shafted flicker sails across an opening to a cottonwood tree branch. Almost immediately, another flicker lands below the first, and they mate.

Well, after all, isn't this what April days are all about?

Spring

For the Birds
🐦

If I think much about it, I recognize that I don't bird watch much any more. Seldom do I go out primarily to look for birds, seldom for more than a brief period. No more deliberate birding outings that start at dawn and go until dark or exhaustion, whichever comes first. Living with a recovering bird watcher exacts a certain acceptance of things-as-they-are.

Yet, here I am, out early for a couple of hours on a mid-April morning. Just me and the puppy. I've an unexpected urge to look for birds. It's hard to take the bird watcher entirely out of some people.

I rounded up the usual suspects while rambling a mile or two along the Snake River: kestrel, mountain bluebird, Barrow's goldeneye, raven, white pelican, chipping sparrow, red-winged blackbird, bald eagle, robin, Canada goose, magpies, some gull whose species I couldn't agree with myself on. Not bad for an amateur.

I've been an amateur this or that pretty much forever. I dabble at things, gain a meager grasp of them, and go on to something new ... computers being one deliberate exception.

Spring

For a variety of reasons, computers don't intrigue me.

Nature does.

I had almost no knowledge of natural history until Meg took over my real education after college. Then, we got into fly fishing, never contemplating for a moment that a person could create a career doing it. With a guy named Dusty Rhodes (has there ever been a male child named Rhodes whose nickname wasn't Dusty?), we invented one of the first fiberglass fly rods ever to whip the air. But we never went anywhere with it. Or, I didn't. I don't know where Dusty is. Probably fishing some place exotic with a casting rod.

I don't know precisely why bird watching has persisted so long as a hobby, despite my having abandoned it several times. I suppose, for me, it's a great excuse to be outdoors. It also compels me, almost literally, to look at other aspects of natural history: weather, seasons, trees, shrubs, streams, ponds, elevations, daily cycles, migration, predator/prey relationship, population dynamics. On and on. No end to fascinating topics, to engrossing subjects. One can concentrate on a particular bird or dynamic and become expert in that, or be a generalist and remain, like me, an amateur.

I enjoy knowing that amateurs can make real contributions to ornithology. My observations—or yours—if valid and carefully made and recorded, are gladly and gratefully made part of the scientific data.

This aspect of bird watching satisfies something fundamentally important to the technical person still lurking inside, albeit deep within.

It's hard to take the scientist entirely out of some people.

And so, fly fishing is behind me. Meteorology. Golf. Geology. Carpentry. Tennis. Chess.

Not all that many pursuits, really, because my work was for a long time satisfying and consuming. That's over, too. Bird watching has remained, ever since a particular osprey, a noisy pair of great blue herons, and an imperturbable American bittern compelled us to go to the library to learn about them.

Besides, when I'm outdoors, looking about, feeling the air, admiring the sky, enjoying the scene, I don't get too introspective. I don't ask, "Why Am I Doing This?" I simply appreciate each opportunity. Glad to be here.

Quiet
❦

One evening in late spring, Meg and I went for a drive. We had no destination or particular purpose. Perhaps just to look around. Perhaps to clear our minds.

We saw a few sagebrush buttercups and yellow fritillaries, a handful of cow buffalo ...

Spring

At one favorite spot we stopped "to let the puppy out," a good excuse I tend to overdo.

And were overwhelmed by a delicious quiet.

We stood with sagebrush in the foreground, the Snake River in the middle ground, the Teton Range — all of it — displayed in the background. Behind us, aspen and a few evergreens. Around us: Silence.

No wind. No vehicle noise. No birds. Too early and cold for insects. No damn airplane noise.

We were reminded of the first time either of us had experienced total quiet. It was near or perhaps just within Big Bend National Park a long time ago. We were 70 miles from any settlement; no airline routes went nearby. We became aware, separately, of a sound — a rushing, swirling periodicity. And then we understood that we each could hear our own blood flowing through, well, arteries, I suppose.

To be sure, this time we didn't hear our blood flowing. Maybe the blood doesn't flow as fast. That first time was a long time ago, and we were hot-blooded then. Factually: It was probably close to 100 degrees that Texas day. On this Wyoming evening going into night, it was closer to 20 degrees.

Maybe we didn't give our senses time to adjust to silence. Maybe we just held/clung on to the wonder of quiet and cherished that more than some renewed sensation.

In any case, we toughed it out until our toes got cold

and the new sound of modern outer clothing rubbing against itself began to intrude.

Nice while it lasted.

Predator...And Pray
❧

I was wool-gathering, I suppose, on this particular spring morning — sauntering along a bank of the Snake River — when I became aware of a bird staring at me. Hard. It was in plain sight, but I knew if it hadn't watched me so intently I'd have passed under it without notice.

Startled, I was even more surprised to identify it as a male peregrine falcon. Handsome devil, to be sure.

He sat as I looked at him from half a dozen angles, up close and personal. He watched me, I admired him. He looked at my puppy in a predatory way, but not seriously; birds are peregrines' staple, supplemented by an occasional ground squirrel or rodent. Hilary never noticed: Cocker spaniels are nose-to-ground oriented.

As I watched the puppy and peregrine I recalled an experience with her immediate predecessor. That cocker had a white coat similar to a snowshoe hare's pelage.

When she was little we called her "owl bait." We went out with her at night to ensure she didn't become a neighborhood great horned owl's dinner.

Spring

That puppy and I were snowshoeing across sage on our way to a stand of cottonwoods that defined the Gros Ventre River when I looked up and noticed a golden eagle hovering above us. It looked down at us—at her. I concluded it might be thinking it had found the biggest doggone snowshoe hare in the valley; I called for the pup to get close to me. Golden eagles can take down sizable ungulates, for heaven's sake. "OOPS, sorry," wouldn't cut it as an apology. I like to think an eagle wouldn't take me on; if it did, I'd be in trouble.

Which brings to mind another incident. It didn't happen in Jackson Hole or elsewhere in the Rockies. However, it is vivid in my recollection. We had camped at a petroglyph site in New Mexico, enjoying the rock art and pretending winter in the Southwest was easier and warmer than winter in Jackson Hole. I had gone out poking around; I wrote about what happened and it goes like this:

"Shambling along, eyes down, tired, distracted by persistent, high gusty, dusty wind. Suddenly, a sure knowledge of being closely watched. Up here? On this ridge? By whom...or what?

"Turkey vulture. No, two turkey vultures.

"Really close, just yards away. Hanging on the wind, tilting back and forth. Hanging there, looking us over."

By this time, the puppy was close, pressing on my leg, protecting me, I'm sure. I watched those ominous silhou-

ettes. Ominous? OK: I'm conditioned by the Western motion pictures of my youth, those scenes in which the lonely
rider sees a kettle of vultures and *knows* what's happened to
Tex or Slim or the school marm. Or the ones where the victims are stretched out on the baking ground by the bad guys,
and the vultures are circling. In those old movies, vultures
seemed to croak in anticipation.

But this puppy hadn't ever seen a Western. (They don't
make 'em like that anymore.) She simply didn't care for the
way those huge black birds loomed over us. Just looking at
us. In silence. Hanging on the stiff wind, floating on huge
wings. Their six-foot wing span measures the same as mine.
I held my arms out, angled them to simulate a vulture's di-
hedral, and gave it a good go. Given my weight I calculated
I'd need arms as long as a football field. And a running
start.

The big buzzards were young birds; their heads black,
not red. Their two-toned wings distinct and distinctive.
They hung near us, eased off, came close again for another
look. Did they know something I should know? Did I look
that weary? That close to falling over?

Turkey vultures are in the clean-up game. They're
strictly carrion eaters and do not hunt prey. I don't doubt
they easily detect when an animal is nearing its end, but
they don't dispatch any. They wait, hang about, and watch.

We fooled them this time. We made it safely back to

the watering hole. Hilary drank water. I had a therapeutic gin-and-tonic.

Everyday Miracles
❦

Early May is an exciting time in Jackson Hole. I had my first sight of newly hatched Canada geese this morning. There are baby bald eagles in the area, although I didn't see any in two nests I inspected from a distance. We did see acre upon acre of yellow fritillary, spring beauty and sage buttercups. Lupine are in leaf, not yet in bloom. Lilacs are ready to pop.

Daffodils, hyacinth and tulips color gardens; balsam root, bluebells and larkspurs dot the wild meadows.

Baby bison indulge in the very few carefree frisks nature permits them.

On my strolls this morning and evening and on our tour around the valley, we notice common nighthawks, double-crested cormorants, ring-billed gulls, sora rails, yellow-rumped warblers, and chipping and vesper sparrows. Other observers have reported varied thrush, black-crowned night heron, yellow-billed sapsuckers, a dickcissel, northern waterthrush, common loons, and Northern orioles.

Early May. A period of excitement, stress, restlessness,

hormonal urges, movement. And that's just in the nature watchers ....

Dry. Meg notices wildflower plants are stunted, shorter in stature albeit blooming. Jackson Hole has been in a dry cycle since the late 1980s. On this May larkspur and narrowleaf balsam root are half their normal height. Big bluegrass is short and already going to seed. Yet, gromwell appears unaffected.

As afternoon light is fading, we watch a female common merganser absolutely slam-dunk herself into her nest hole in a cottonwood tree. She cruises at 35 mph up to the very last possible moment ... an everyday, Olympic, performance.

On our way home we are privileged to watch a spectacular moonrise. An enormous full moon, rising with seeming buoyancy over the Gros Ventre Mountains.

Just your average monthly miracle.

Lupine

80

Spring Magic
❦

On a certain day in May, a day which can be anytime the first two weeks, spring explodes into full frenzy. Leaves appear, seemingly in just a couple of hours. Grass and shrubs turn from dull brown to bright green. Birds sing and chase around and occupy every possible niche. Not to mention a few unlikely ones. Animals — including humans — respond, each in idiosyncratic ways.

This particular animal anticipates the day, the hour, when new aspen leaves not yet fully opened cover the hillsides with a certain haze, a hue of soft green light — and then makes sure to go out and ramble, if only for an hour.

Some years that's as long as spring gets to be. I remember one year spring was on Tuesday, about 2:30 p.m.. By nightfall it was summer. Long or short, spring is a magical time. (Long is better.)

Yesterday's bare ground is a field of wildflowers today. Empty skies fill with insects, followed immediately by insectivorous birds. Hibernating animals re-appear. Baby wild creatures make their entrances.

Short-sleeve shirts appear under down vests. Sap rises. Sap flows. Saps get sunburns. A few aches and pains ameliorate.

Spring

Other parts of the continent have longer, more spectacular springs. More flowers, flowering shrubs, flowering trees. By the time spring comes to Jackson Hole, it's over pretty much everywhere else.

Thus, an urgent season becomes frenetic. Time's wasting. All at once there's a new insect, a bird returning, a wildflower popping up, a newly bare mountain slope, a thunderstorm, cumulus clouds: A tumult of sight and sound, color and the throb of life.

One Moment in May
❦

Mid-May marks the peak of bird migration in these parts, give or take a week one way or another.

On this particular mid-May morning our bird feeder held a male lazuli bunting, Cassin's finches, a pair of black-headed grosbeaks, a dark-eyed junco, and a western tanager — all at one time. A close-by tree hosted evening grosbeaks, pine siskins, and a yellow-headed blackbird. What a pretty sight.

And what colors! Luscious turquoise blue, yellow-brown, orange-brown, blacks, whites, reds, shades of gray.

Birds were particularly eager to get to the feeder this day, a day after a Rocky Mountain spring snowstorm. Such storms are regular May events in Jackson Hole. (And in

June some years ... not to mention early July.) Especially in May, storms force spring migrant birds to layover near snow-free stream edges and roadsides. Sometimes astonishing numbers of sparrows, bluebirds, blackbirds, siskins, long-spurs and horned larks are seen the first nice day following a spring snowstorm, providing the best clues to the kinds and numbers of birds on the move during North American migration periods. Thousands of birds per mile of road-way, for many miles.

I'm grateful a few of them favored our feeder, however they got here. I watched them for quite a while, investing my time wisely on this spring morning.

Ungulates
❦

I guess it's too late for me to study biology seriously — or any other discipline or field but I've thought it would be interesting to try to understand ungulate hoofs, and how and why they differ among themselves. This passing fancy occurred after Meg and I watched several bighorn sheep trip gaily down a snow-covered talus slope — only to slow to an exaggerated tiptoe, cautious, discomforting slow dance across a macadam road surface. Once across, they rapidly and confidently scaled the opposite rock face.

Moose, on the other hand, avoid steep traverses and macadam. Deer seem comfortable on pavement—and get clobbered on the highways in appalling numbers. I don't know what pigs do on tarmac or concrete; someone must have studied that, surely. (If not, there's my master's thesis ...)

Camels need differently constructed hooves, I'm certain, than do horses. The hoof, as I understand it, covers the ends of ungulate digits. Do I actually comprehend digits on horses and buffalo? Nope.

Ought to study it.

Gee! Get a degree and become an animal podiatrist.

Naw.

Leader of the pack
❦

Sometimes I walk the puppy in town on a well-used (read: often abused) piece of open ground. It's OK for dogs to be there, and it's easy for me to keep an eye on her.

Lots of people use this area for all sorts of activities, some of which I'd rather not know. There are clues should I want to inquire; but I really don't. I do know people eat stuff there because the tell-tale morning residue is unmistakable: bits of burger, pieces of pizza, wrappings from fast food franchises. The foundation of modern littering.

Usually a few ravens and magpies are patrolling each

morning, searching for anything interesting and edible. For a number of years I watched, on and off, one particular raven, a large bird with a distinctive habit of hop-skipping. A female, I supposed, because of its size.

This bird's duty, it seemed, was to be the first to approach and touch a promising or irresistible, but possibly dangerous, object. The first one to pick up a crumpled bag or piece of wrapping. The first one to discover how to shake out a bit of food or turn over a plate. A maven raven, showing eager companions how to do things, pointing the way.

Leader of the pack.

Summer

Welcome Back, Summer
❦

Today is the first day of summer. I take my clue from the western wood-pewee. When that flycatcher returns and begins to call, it's summer for me, no matter what the sun or calendar says.

On my stroll this morning, I was in late spring, accompanied by groups of western tanagers, mourning doves, yellow-headed blackbirds, a pair of redhead ducks and yellow warblers. I'd gone perhaps two-thirds of a mile when—from a stand of narrow-leaf cottonwoods—came the unmusical, insect-like *pecurrr* note of this, my personal signal bird.

I had walked into summer.

Oh, I know, I know. But summer is an attitude as much as a season. I've been in fierce valley snowstorms on July 4, the beginning of two weeks of bitter cold, wet weather that killed nesting birds and young animals.

Summer? Not to me. It wasn't even spring.

It was late winter.

Western wood-pewees seem to me — I have no field data to substantiate this — to wait deliberately until a good, steady supply of summer insects is assured before returning. When they, ah, sing, I call it summer.

So sue me.

Soon, too soon, that nasal *peeurrr* will recede into the background noise of summer, barely distinguishable from many similar sounds. Nature's Muzak™, elevator sounds: It's there, but not remarkable.

The flip side of this start of summer will be, all too soon, the end. One day, very early in September, I'll be outdoors in wood-pewee habitat and be vaguely ill-at-ease. It will occur to me that the western wood-pewee no longer calls.

Then my summer will be over.

Oh, there will be hot days yet in the year. The sun still powerful, a few birds still nesting, some even starting families. But summer is over.

Today I simply call my call up into the trees: "Welcome back. Thanks for summer."

Across the Great Divide
❦

I live west of the Continental Divide.

The Continental Divide is a hydrographic distinction: Rivers flowing east of the divide eventually end up in the

Atlantic Ocean. Those flowing west of it end up in the Pacific. Distinction or not, unless you're another Captain William Clark-- the Clark of Lewis and Clark who possessed an uncanny ability to recognize the lay of the land—you might walk over the hump of the continent in these parts and entirely miss both its presence and significance. The Divide, however, is real and palpable; it's worth seeking out and recognizing.

The Continental Divide is one of many reasons wildlife habitat varies so where I live. Its geology demarks both dramatic and subtle changes in climate, forest types, topography, susceptibility to air stagnation episodes—and air pollution—and animal migration patterns.

In the Rocky Mountains, the Continental Divide runs roughly northwest to southeast. It is never, ever, in a straight line. Jackson, Wyoming, is west of the Divide, as is all of Grand Teton National Park. Red Lodge and West Yellowstone, Montana, and Cody, Wyoming, are east of it. The Divide splits Yellowstone National Park: Yellowstone Lake and Old Faithful Geyser Basin are on the east side, the Snake River and its tributaries on the west.

In the Teton Wilderness lies a creek whose waters themselves divide, a portion flowing to the Atlantic, the remainder to the Pacific—appropriately called Two Ocean Creek.

The Divide may be imperceptible or dramatic. It may go unnoticed from the windows of a powerful vehicle or the back of a horse. It rests at 9,000 feet in most of the Greater Yellowstone Ecosystem, climbing to a high point of just under 11,000 feet on Beartooth Pass near the Montana/Wyoming border.

Elevation affects wildlife habitat as much as the Divide itself. Cody, Wyoming, is 5,000 feet; heck, corn actually grows and matures there. Red Lodge is 5,550 feet. Dubois, Wyoming, is 6,900 feet, but has a milder climate than Jackson at 6,200 feet, the result of rain and snow "shadows" cast by the Tetons.

Thermal areas, differing soils, lakes and rivers all affect plants and animals.

I try in my wanderings to be alert to these and other influences. In general: North-facing slopes, river edges (and sidewalks) keep their snowpack longer than slopes with other aspects; Douglas fir, spruce and lodgepole forests tend to grow on them. South-facing slopes are often shrub-covered — "bare" in the vernacular. It's cooler year-round on north-facing slopes. Meadows lush at 8,500 feet are dry and sere at 6,000 feet, other factors being roughly equal. Sagebrush steppes are arid and harsh, as are alpine regions.

Large tracts of unbroken lodgepole pine forests occur where I live. They're usually quiet places without a rich and varied wildlife population. Alpine tundra also tends to harbor a limited spectrum of animals and plants. Ponds, lake edges and river bottoms provide excellent wildlife habitat

for animals large and small. In nature almost no niche remains in *vacuo*, but some habitats are distinctly more viable
than others in supporting a diversity of wildlife species.

Sometimes I use my knowledge to improve the odds of
finding wildlife, deliberately directing my outings to aspen
woodlands or river edges or areas I know a certain animal
prefers. This is useful when taking a census of bald eagles
or trumpeter swans, searching for pocket gophers, checking
the spawning frenzy of rosy-sided suckers—thought to be
declining locally—or gathering some other needed information.

I enjoy such times. But it is my general custom simply
to get out when I can and make quiet observations of whatever I'm fortunate to recognize.

And only then to figure out which side of the Divide I
find myself.

Trees
❦

A tree, if lucky enough to have been left alone by man,
is where it is, and indeed what it is, by having won a serious
struggle for survival. Competition for success—that is to
say, life and maturity—among plants is unremitting and
complex and as hard as it can be for any living thing. Trees
can't migrate to avoid heat or drought or cold. They have to
find suitable moisture, soil, sunlight, shade, climate, expo-

sure, and luck against an unending army of enemies — deliberate or unknowing — rooted in place.

I talk to trees. I whisper them good fortune. I pat them. I admire them. I know they hurt when they're assaulted and I mourn for them when that happens. I'm going to keep

Douglas Fir

doing all this as long as I can, or until they begin to talk back to me and I don't like what they're saying. I have certain limits, after all.

I like trees. I don't recall ever being uncomfortable in a forest; I assume trees are my friends. But, I've been uneasy in the middle of cities on sunny afternoons.

Yet, I've killed my share of trees.

We've almost always lived in wood houses with wood tables and chairs and other furnishings. One house required that trees be cut down to accommodate it, the driveway and infrastructure. We replaced all we could but — bottom line — created a net loss. In our search for survival, comfort and security, we became enemies of trees.

There was a time — hell, we're still apparently in it — when trees were considered the worst enemy faced on this continent by conquering Caucasian Man. Forests were destroyed, for it was dark in there. Devils, if not the Devil himself, lurked inside. Howls and other mysterious, forbidding sounds came from the woods. An opening wouldn't do; all the trees had to be removed. Indians could creep up otherwise ...

Even today, we accept the notion that a "security light" does more than destroy the night with a peculiar glare: It keeps the infernals away. Yeah, right.

Trees did doggone well on this continent before white man. Read any of the journals of early explorations. Now trees are gone in many places, going in most of the rest. I'll make a pact with you: I won't attempt to go into photosynthesis, or sap conduction, or the difference between deciduous and evergreen trees, or strategies of seed dispersion, or the role of fire. In exchange, you plant some trees.

Also, now and again, pet a tree. Say "Hi."

Beetles
🐞

Ahead on the path is a young deer mouse. Dead. Dead, but still moving.

It's moving in the recycling dance, heaving and writhing in rigid mime, as carrion beetles and other organisms carry it away, doing a seldom celebrated clean-up that makes the planet habitable.

I forego close examination in favor of figuring out how this particular mouse died. There's no obvious reason, no sign of attack. A superficially intact animal.

The young of many species suffer stunning mortality rates. In his supercilious fashion, man considers the survival rate of other animals — if he does at all — in terms of his own interest. And mice? Generally in terms of man's convenience.

I wonder why a raven, coyote, weasel, magpie or some other predator didn't find such an obvious corpse before the beetles did. I conclude, tentatively, that I underrate beetles.

Odd, to underrate them. Close to 30,000 species are known to live in the United States alone; there are probably 10 times that many species worldwide. They're found in almost every habitat on the planet, and range in size from minuscule creatures to critters measuring over four inches in length: Ones you could throw a saddle on and ride.

The carrion beetles on the mouse are just over an inch in length and dark — almost black — with prominent reddish-orange markings on their forewings. I can't tell if the mouse carcass is moving because the beetles are excavating dirt underneath it or moving the mouse off the trail to a moister, shadier place; for concealment; or some other reason known only to them.

My investigation is partly cut short by the puppy getting entirely too interested in the matter — but mostly because I'm unequipped emotionally and, ah, surgically to look closer. When we returned an hour later, the mouse's carcass has been moved roughly its own length off the trail. Impressive.

Carrion Beetle

97

Summer

In June it's entirely too easy to find dead animals: Animals killed by motor vehicles, fledgling birds killed by crashing into windows, ungulates young and old struck down after being mesmerized by headlights. Nature is constantly testing and challenging and probing with her arsenal of predators, disease, pests, weather, accident and chance.

Two days later I don't find a trace of the little deer mouse or the carrion beetles that disposed of it.

Nest Housekeeping
❦

Robins usually nest under our deck, building nests on a secluded, shaded horizontal span. They're welcome. They're such delightful signs of spring when they arrive, and so dang purposeful: Arriving one day, building nests the next.

I've noticed many times that while I often hear robin song, I've never witnessed much in the way of courtship — not to mention actual copulation. Every bird watcher has witnessed copulation in one bird species or another: in waterfowl (mallard ducks are notoriously amorous), in domestic fowl, in bigger birds like hawks or ravens. Some biologists — and many of my best friends are biologists — go to great lengths to document mating in species they are moni-

toring. Robin mating doesn't get much play in the literature. I guess it's not a big deal to the robins.

Come to reflect on it, there are biologists who perform
the darndest things in their studies. There's literally no ori-
fice unexplored or unremarked upon in biologists' lexicon.
Nothing is sacred in what passes for science these days.

I digress.

This June morning a robin flies off its nest, carrying
something white in its bill. I know it's a fecal sac. Songbird
nestlings, confined as they are to their nest, void their excrement in small, whitish sacs. Parents remove these tough,
mucous membrane-wrapped tidy packages from the nest,
carrying them some distance before disposing.

Robins seems to scatter their offspring's offerings in
wide arcs. One friend watched a male Brewer's blackbird
deliberately and repeatedly drop his babies' fecal sacs in a
stream. She netted and examined a number of them, noting
that each was pinched closed with a little black-tipped,
twisted seal. Neat observation. Neat disposal system.

I wonder if the seal is made clockwise. Maybe some
biologist did his master's study on this.

Biologists have examined the general topic of elimina-
tion of birds in some detail. They've discovered that birds
of prey lift their tails and eject excrement immediately before taking off from their perch. The health of a bird can be,
in fact, judged by the distance from its perch, or especially

the nest, it propels its excrement. Sick birds are unable to avoid fouling their situation. When not in their nest, song-birds and other bird species deposit their whitish droppings beneath them—whether perched, on the ground, or in the air.

Biologists have summarized their findings, calling some birds "shooters," others "dribblers." At certain biologist meetings and conventions, restrooms are identified by those descriptive terms. It always gets a laugh.

Field biology can be a lonely business.

Warbler removing fecal sac

Snakes and Toads

❧

I'm glad there are no poisonous snakes or other dangerously toxic critters in Jackson Hole. (As a student of natural history, I should be inclined to say that no poisonous snakes have so far been reported. But, what the heck.) Immediately outside of the valley one finds poisonous snakes; I've always been alert to that possibility, yet to date I've recognized only four live ones, even "outside."

One spring morning, years ago, I was astonished to come upon a mating ball of garter snakes. All I did was walk 50 steps from my car—not a tough observation. They were on macadam, which felt 15 degrees warmer than adjacent ground.

A phone call came this day from a rafter who "found" a two-foot long rubber boa in the Snake River Canyon.

Who found whom? The constrictor wrapped around his arm and demonstrated why it's known as a constrictor. Boas can reach nine feet, at which length their capability might not be so easily dismissed. My brave correspondent enjoyed this encounter and gently released his acquaintance.

I wouldn't try to guess how many snakes I've overlooked and missed seeing. Frankly, I hope the snakes and I continue our mutual overlooking and ignoring. I'll do my part.

Walking this morning along a major dike that parallels miles of the Snake River, I come upon a squashed western toad. Recent studies point out — warn, actually — of serious decline in amphibian populations worldwide; I pick this toad up to give to some authority. It isn't endangered: It's dead. Its species, if still extant, is seriously threatened. Why the hell did this creature happen to be in a tire track at the wrong moment on the wrong day? I'm angry at the driver. At the toad, too.

Which is foolish. I put the sentiment aside.

Further down the dike I spy a tiger salamander. Common, but most visitors and residents never see one. We have been privileged to know two old-timers born in the valley. He had the distinction of being the first white, male child born in Jackson Hole, in the late 1800's.

He did everything that could be done outdoors, yet never saw a salamander on his own. She gardened all her life on a plain often flooded by Flat Creek; she never saw one, either. We were pleased to show them both this creature — and are still amazed we late comers were the ones to do so.

By 10 a.m. on this July day it's already warm. I've had enough of snakes and toads. I head for home.

Dead
❦

A small brown animal lies dead beneath an evergreen tree 20 feet from our kitchen steps. Slim, long body, maybe 10 inches from head to tail. On close examination I see its top is brownish, its underside almost white. It has little white feet.

A short-tailed weasel, killed by something. Its throat is ripped out; its tail is in two pieces, the black-tip neatly separated. Yet, scavengers haven't touched it.

Was it killed in a fight? By another weasel? By an active pocket gopher? A ground squirrel? No, they've been underground for weeks now. A cat? Why would a cat simply leave it? Was this dead ermine young and inexperienced? Did it simply make a mistake? I don't know.

The corpse is out in the open, quite far from the tree's trunk; I'm surprised a raven or magpie hasn't made a meal of it. It's been warm and dry this summer, and this once graceful animal is desiccated and hard to the touch. Oddly, it remains graceful even in rigor.

Where our house is located, we don't often see weasels in any season. I never saw this one alive. My loss.

The ground is hot and dry and hard. It takes a little while to make a grave.

Color

Trumpeter swans are white. A rather brilliant white. They can be distinguished even when flying low against snow-covered background; they stand out against darker backgrounds.

White and bright signifies the presence of little if any pigment; all visible light wave lengths that fall on the birds are reflected, a definition of white. It also means the structure of trumpeter feathers scatters the wave lengths in such manner that the reflected light is brilliant.

In contrast, the quality of scattered and reflected light from the underside of a mountain chickadee is less brilliant — a hue we call gray.

The black bill of the trumpeter swan is black because it absorbs all visible light wave lengths. This results in an absence of color, what we call black. When some wave lengths are absorbed but others reflected we see, separately, yellow, blue and red — the red lip mark of the trumpeter.

In art one is concerned with the primary colors yellow, blue and red, and with white and black. (I have learned this, to the extent I know it, from aquarellist Fred Kingwill and from my Art Critic. It hasn't been easy.) In bird feathers, however, there's not only pigmentary color—dependent upon light reflection and light absorption—but also this structural color business, in which light is reflected, scattered or masked by the tiny ridges and grooves of their feathers. Each miniscule structure behaves like a prism, separating light into component colors and creating the optical illusion of iridescence.

Structural color is responsible for the wonderful blues of mountain bluebirds, for all the blues and all the whites

Trumpeter swan and cygnets

that birds exhibit. It's responsible for the iridescence in hummingbird plumage, for the green-black shimmer in magpies, and for purples in jays. I read somewhere that a pinion jay's feather immersed in alcohol — destroying its light scattering ability — appears black. If I should ever have a blue feather and alcohol I want to devote to such casual and non-consumptive use, I intend to prove or disprove that fact.

While structural color is important, most of the colors birds exhibit is pigmentary color created by organic compounds. Browns, blacks, grays, yellows and pinks result from melanins, the same compounds that color human hair and skin. Pyrrolic pigments (porphyrins) are responsible for greens, reds, and browns; carotenoids for yellows, oranges and reds.

In breeding season, a male mallard displays a rainbow of pigmentary and structural colors: green and iridescent green head; yellow bill; orange feet; brilliant white neck band; a rich mixture of red and brown on its breast; gray-brown-black back and wings; iridescent blue to purple speculum bordered by brilliant white; a soft white and gray underbelly; and a sporty black-and-white tail assembly. Nifty. On close inspection, birds are colorful people.

Why? That's another story. Plumage colors and patterns are important for species recognition, display, courtship and protection.

Whatever works.

Summer

Water

❦

I like the various sounds of running water. Murmurs and bubbling, swishing and tumbling noises — even the ominous, deeper background sounds of flood stage rivers. In my part of the world, river bottoms are cobble-lined; fast, high water brings a *clickiting* or *clackiting* as rock is carried along and eroded, accompanied by a tearing sound as uprooted trees and plant debris are transported to some new repose. The reverberation is superimposed upon an unsettling sensation felt through one's feet and teeth.

On winter days, there's the different sound of ice rubbing upon ice — a tearing and abrading, but not abrasive sound. It's natural music. It belongs. Belongs to the season, to the river.

I like to look at running water, particularly clean running water. Clean standing water — water I can look *into*, not just at. In much of this continent, the water in rivers, ponds, creeks and lakes is so muddy and contaminated it's no longer transparent. At one time I had to think about, deal with, and look at, dirty water. Meg and I vacationed in Jackson Hole back then. I spent happy hours simply looking into clean water, a pleasure we were denied most of the year.

It's unfortunate that even though my favorite waters are clear, I typically can't see what I know to be there. I've accepted that good fly fishermen and skillful river runners see fish and underwater rocks; I never can. They have a gift — practice hasn't helped me. I'm content, as there is no choice, to imagine what is concealed. I know trout feed on lines revealed by surface patterns. I know they are in pools and close to lakeshores. I know there are aquatic insects, not to mention plants.

I don't see them. Oh, a duck, perhaps, or a mink — should I have especially good luck — but not some log waiting to grab at anything I might be floating past upon.

I'm not much at being in water, either. I might feel dif-

ferently if wading boots came anywhere near my size. Or if I could swim. Or if I just liked the feel of water.

I'm simply entirely happy to look at gin-clear water. Water-clear gin is pretty nice to contemplate, too.

Green
❦

Summer solstice occurred not quite two weeks ago. It is everywhere green. The green of wild rose and alfalfa, of pussytoe leaves and gilia, of blue flax and balsamroot. The green of full summer, accented by yellows, reds, blues, and diminishing brown hues. Invigorating greens. Promising greens. Productive greens.

I think of it as the pinnacle green, the apex green. If I weren't trying so hard to be so cutesy, the just-at-the-start-of-autumn green. The green-before-the-chlorophyll-shuts-off-green. The green that suggests you ought to do at least some of the things you absolutely had to get done this summer...some left over from previous years.

It's a nourishing green, welcomed by the young and old elk and cow, deer and pika, ground squirrel and snowshoe hare. It's the gardener's green. The tourist's green. The hiker's green. The artist's green. The green-to-hang-onto-green.

Because soon enough, it will be brown.

109

Blowin' In The Wind
🌱

This morning, up through the long strand of cottonwood trees that line the Snake River in its meander through Jackson Hole, unimaginable numbers of cottonwood seeds were being shed. Uncountable numbers of seeds carried along on filaments, or hairs, called pappi. Incomprehensible numbers of seeds engaged in the act of reproduction, of dispersal. Cast upon the wind, given over to chance.

Windrows of seeds ensconced in "cotton" piled up in ground hollows, against obstacles, floated on the river and ponds, lined the water edges. Ankle-deep drifts of cotton, dustings of white defining the path, a fuzz drifting through the air. On the ground, in the air, festooning a big, old poplar.

I scuffed along, stirring up seeds, trampling great quantities, wondering what the odds were that any one seed is viable, any one will sprout, any one produce a surviving, seed-producing cottonwood. I can't fathom such odds. Zero, maybe; no, not zero. I picked some up, examined them under my trusty hand lens. Not zero—but I wouldn't bet the ranch on the few in my hand. I put them down in an hospitable place. Maybe I tilted the odds. I doubt it.

Pollens of all sorts were abroad. Certainly enough to satisfy every one sensitive or allergic to such things. The sight of clouds of pine pollen drifting out of, over, and beyond stands of forest was a sight to marvel at. To enjoy. To flee, perhaps. Megamillions, megabillions of tiny seeds each off on its journey, hostage to the vagaries of wind direction and velocity, to the whim of chance. And to luck.

By chance I was out at the peak of seed dispersal for these particular cottonwood trees. Chance. And luck.

Gardeners and Gatherers
❦

Jackson Hole provides much to sustain the soul but relatively little to sustain the palate. Gardening is iffy. It can frost any day of the year, so one may be limited to potatoes, carrots, onions and perhaps peas, spinach and lettuce. Not bad, but it ain't fresh corn and tomatoes.

Growing naturally in the Hole are various edible, choice mushrooms and an assortment of wild berries and seeds: huckleberries, grouse whortleberries, rose hips, and chokecherry, among others.

There are successful gardeners here. There are successful gatherers. Successful gardeners and gatherers flaunt bags, baskets and trays full of edibles. We've actually, in our time here, known people who produce quantities of veg-

111

etables, people who go off into the woods and fields and return with bags of mushrooms. They look like regular people. We privately suspect they may be space aliens.

Why? Because, of course, we're lousy gardeners and worse gatherers. At least when we gardened, we knew with reasonable precision where we'd planted seed and sets. In the wild, however, we searched with diligence and a certain amount of persistence for mushrooms, let's say, and on our best day, between us, returned with a dozen. Later we saw pick-up trucks carrying full plastic bags of delectable fungi others found that very day.

There are localities named Huckleberry This or Huckleberry That. Must be some reason for those names. We've

Huckleberries

never gone home with as much as a quart of berries.

We've given up gardening. And mushrooming. They involve bending over or down and getting up again. Do we begrudge those who have fresh veggies, snow mushrooms and morels?

A little.

Parched
❧

Who would've predicted that as the 20th Century staggers to its end (in 2001 ... but that's another no-win discourse) everyone, everywhere would have a water bottle — reminiscent of a baby's feeding bottle — always at hand? Not me, that's certain.

On the trail, in the car, at the movies, in the classroom or lecture hall, at home, on the ski slope, on the picnic beach, strapped to the bicycle, tucked in backpack or hung on the belt.

Ubiquitous. Even on baby carriages, where they seem most comfortable.

In this milieu it seems almost unthinkable that Meg and I once got caught without water so long we pretty much went bonkers. In our defense, let me say we'd been lulled into a false sense of comfort back at a time when it was OK to drink the waters in high mountain creeks. We carried a cup, and entertained no further consideration. This was before giardia lurked in every teaspoon of sparkling stream — and when streams trickled throughout the summer.

So, on a promising summer day, eons ago, we hiked up

113

Death Canyon Trail in Grand Teton National Park to look at rocks, at sky, at wildlife, at wildflowers, at our park. We expected a hot day; we got a HOT day. By early afternoon, somewhere above a patch of extraordinarily tall horse mint, we were anxious to find water.

There was none to be found. Or, that we could find.

I know now we weren't thinking clearly. We were suffering from dehydration, which affected our ability to reason. There may indeed have been water nearby—I can't doubt it—but we found only dry watersheds.

We did know enough to seek shade and then to head downslope. Death Canyon seemed more aptly named with each passing quarter-hour. Talk about *hot*.

Broiling. Fierce. All-encompassing. Hot rocks, radiating from below, from the sides, and for all we could tell, above. Debilitating heat.

A stroll had become, in our minds — our febrile minds — a death march. Feeble jokes to that effect were exceedingly transparent. We were in a hot oven being roasted. Alone. Nobody else had been silly enough to subject himself to this trail on this day.

Near the end, Meg crawled under an overhang and curled up in the shade, announcing that it had been nice knowing me and all that, but she was going to remain there forever. So long, kid. The only argument she responded favorably to was that our cocker spaniel was waiting for us

114

on the valley floor. Needed us, depended on us. We had to get down. For her.

We slowly stumbled down to the parking lot, drank from the big jug we once thought too cumbersome to carry, petted the puppy, recovered. Cooled off by the time evening came. Hydrated before dark. Unfried our brains. Figger'd we might wait until cooler weather to take that particular trail again. Bought a canteen. Learned a couple of things.

And, back then, bounced back. On another trail in a couple of days. With water.

Fish Stories

One summer Meg caught so many lake trout in a cove on the west side of Jackson Lake that it was temporarily known as Meg's Cove among the jealous and covetous — the average fishermen, that is.

Of course, it never happened there or that way again. Not to her or to us, anyhow. Not that we didn't try.

On one later try, in another June, we witnessed a natural history spectacular: Utah suckers all dolled up in rosy spawning coloration, having themselves quite an orgy. Lake surface is ordinarily liquid — placid or stirred up — but not comprised of the backs, sides and occasionally bellies of good-sized fish going at it. It was so comprised that morning.

I don't know how to begin to estimate how many suckers were in our view to the front, to the left, to the right and beyond the sandy beach where they'd concentrated. Ten thousand? Fifty thousand? At least. Did they come and go? We still don't know.

We sat and marveled, fishing poles put aside.

We ate lunch, sat and watched, watched and sat, until the sun went behind the mountains and a refreshing coolness blessed the shore. The suckers were still going, but we had, finally, seen enough. (How much raw sexual imperative can a person watch in one sitting, after all?)

We used to fish the rivers and creeks, too. Little creeks, such as Game Creek, big rivers like the Snake. We fished to fish — more than to keep — even though it was a lot easier to catch fish than it is nowadays: Fishing pressure from professionals and amateurs both has vastly increased. We seldom failed to raise a trout, seldom got skunked.

Or so I recall. Memory can be, well, shaded.

The head of the Snake River Canyon, below the confluence with the Hoback River, was a favorite fishing spot. That was when we could scramble down, and back up, steep cobble stream banks — even without a rope tied to a car's bumper to help the process. (Then, cars had bumpers one could tie on to.) Heck, if we ever got down to the river now, we'd have to hike to a flat place where we could climb on a raft and float out, or where a helicopter could land to fly us back out. Even way back, Meg one time got halfway up and couldn't go up or down. Stuck. It wasn't funny ... until some time later.

One of the last times we fished the Snake, we and another couple were standing in two feet of swift water flycasting, not catching anything, when a badger came swimming towards us. Never had seen a badger swimming before. Never particularly wanted to see one, especially in that situation. We gave him a whole lot of room to come ashore, shake, and amble off.

Couple of fish stories, probably obligatory in this genre. I won't tell you about the one that got away.

Marmots
🍂

The calendar says early August. I might not have guessed even close to that date ... Today seems unclassifiable. I decide to call it just-barely-pre-marmot-hibernation-time.

All spring and summer I've watched a marmot pair become a marmot family. The male atypically dark brown, the female a light brown. According to the textbooks they should be yellow-brown with — don't be shocked now — yellow bellies. They should have white fur between the eyes and a buff ruff, or neck patch. Neither of these adults comes close to matching those classic descriptions.

Summer

I haven't seen either adult for 10 days. Their litter of six typically marked yellow-bellied marmots is still abroad. They look just like the drawings. Isn't genetics wonderful?

This morning all six youngsters are out on rocks soaking up a miserably cold morning fog. All plump, healthy-looking, compatible. All inexperienced. Perched above them, only 30 or 40 yards away, is an immature bald eagle.

Well! Interesting. What will happen?

Nothing happens.

Did these young marmots know instinctively that bald eagles prefer other prey, that this bird was also inexperienced, that there was no danger? Surely marmots know danger can come from above. Would they have similarly reacted to a golden eagle, immature or not?

Marmots are common residents of this area, from valley floor to rather high elevations. Apparently, lying asleep on exposed rock in proximity to potential predators has a survival benefit I haven't figured out.

Investments
❦

I have invested innumerable hours looking into the clear water one finds in the Rocky Mountains. Wisely spent hours.

To look into a creek and see cobbles or rocks, fish, aquatic insects or plants, is a joy. To step into it and find it several times deeper than one expects is — well, anywhere from a pleasant surprise to a shock.

I have wisely spent many hours sky-gazing. Looking at the deep blue one needs, can find in too few places, on too few occasions.

Looking at clouds. At summer cumulus and winter nimbostratus. At jet stream cirrus and lenticular altocumulus. At sunrise and sunset. At crepuscular rays and sundogs. At sunrises and sunsets. At the moon and the Milky Way.

The bottom line for these investments? The value of this portfolio? Well, if you have to ask...

Laying In The Wood
❦

The abrupt, albeit expected, silencing and migration of the western wood-pewee is the surest sign summer is over. Another is the increasingly frequent pick-up truck coming down from the forests into town, bearing oversize loads of firewood. At first — even in June — there are one or two trucks; by mid-August, a steady stream. Laying in the wood.

Laying in the wood was, formerly, one of our most pleasant activities. It is a regret, a constant burr under our saddles, that our "wooding" days are done. The thing is, it was never a "must" for us to get our own wood. It was a fun thing to do for us. We usually went with at least one other couple, made a day of it, made a picnic of it, enjoyed being outdoors and feeding horse flies and mosquitoes. There was an element of danger from chain saws and falling trees that was a cautionary undercurrent, but really — we enjoyed it. Fortunately, so did numerous other couples we knew: We almost never went wooding by ourselves. Why, once we even inveigled a house guest to come along, and got a lot of work out of him.

He didn't come back for 11 years.

I suppose it was both the work and preparation we enjoyed: saw blade sharpening, small engine tune-up, water, lunch box, gasoline, oil, a trailer. We actually made a neighborhood trailer with a hefty carrying capacity. Bumbling or not, we certainly *looked* as if we knew what we were doing.

We've had easy wooding — the year after a blow-down and again after fires in Yellowstone. We've also had to build a few roads to get at suitable trees.

And, oh, I know that sometimes when we were pooped and sweaty we wondered why this was fun. But when split and stacked, the wood was satisfying to look upon, to know it was there.

Wood fires are welcoming and warm and, sometimes, the sole heat in the house.

Often, an old-timer would come wooding with us. She

and her husband didn't use their fireplace — she just liked to get out and do some heavy work. She enjoyed it and missed wooding when she couldn't hack it anymore. So do we.

Sunset
🍒

A mid-August evening. We're on an east bank of the Snake River, looking at the water, cottonwood-blue spruce habitat, the Tetons. And, for some time, at a deep, deepening peach-going-to-deep red sunset. Making the mountains glow, staining the river until it runs russet. Getting richer and deeper, first a few clouds touched rust and orange, then the entire horizon.

Suddenly, quietly, it's all gone to gray and a washed-out indigo sky. The spectacle took a half hour, an hour, or no time at all. Or, forever, in the mind.

At our vehicle 40 minutes later, we're joined by a young couple, a hand-in-hand young couple who do the obligatory pet-the-puppy-thing. (The puppy insists on this.)

Then, their faces aglow, they asked, rather breathlessly, "Did you see the sunset? Wasn't it wonderful?"

Yes, we sure did. It sure was. Good for them.

Good for us.

121

Summer

A Good Day
❦

A summer hike around or near Two Ocean and Emma
Matilda lakes was a longed-for ritual with us at one time.
Someone, after all, had to feed the mosquitoes and biting
flies, and the area was usually devoid of people. Oh, a local
couple quietly fishing, perhaps. One year, we saw busy sea-
sonal workers trying to eradicate pine bark beetles with an
insecticide spray probably harmless to the beetles and hurt-
ful to everything else. We avoided the lakes for a couple of
years thereafter.

One hot and still August day we went to Two Ocean
with a couple whose friendship we cherished. She was a
literal old-timer, he was an immigrant from Greece. Charm-
ing people. Our plan was to spend a summer afternoon looking at scenery, animals, whatever might come along, and
then have a picnic.

We had supplies — hamburger, rolls, onion, chips — and
a little fiery Greek beverage and cheese.

It turned out our Greek friend had never eaten a hot
dog. When he made the fire, he made it big enough to cook

an ox. A roaring great, leaping fire, in woods composed mostly of pine bark beetle-killed standing lodgepole pine. Embers rose and drifted up; my heart sank and drifted lower.

It all worked out. No forest fires. Well-cooked burgers and roasted hot dogs. Toasted rolls and toasts to a good day. We drowned the fire exceedingly carefully, got back to their house about 10 p.m., and drank coffee and laughed until after midnight. A good summer day.

Edge of Autumn
❧

A lovely summer morning, a morning balanced on the edge of autumn.

Light frost edges leaves and blades of shrub and grass; in particular, it sees to me, cinquefoil leaves are most clearly outlined with the frost, each vein defined.

An ephemeral definition.

On sunny summer days in the Rockies, temperatures vary dramatically. A 50 or 60 degree swing on a given day isn't unusual, or much remarked upon. Yet it ought to be. Twenty-five degree mornings to 75 or 85 degree afternoons are one of those commonplace miracles in nature easily overlooked. This minor phenomenon accounts, however, for the chance to walk about early on sunny days with few insects to annoy. It accounts for careful footwear choices on those mornings. Old-timers used to complain vociferously about having wet feet all summer, followed by cold feet the rest of the year.

The temperature variance accounts for people walking about wearing short-sleeve shirts and shorts on 25 degree mornings, opting for comfort later in the day over a touch of chilblains early on.

It's why summer is — and has to be — frenetic. An overnight frost induced torpor counterbalanced by a daytime hustle-and-bustle. A hurrying to flower and to set seed, a hurrying to find a mate and reproduce, a hurrying to try to accomplish all that needs to be done, should be done, things one yearns to do and get done, in summer.

Frost-lined cinquefoil leaves

Summer

There's never enough summer in the Rockies. One more week, one more day; summer is abrupt.

Here it is, barely 9 a.m. and the frost already has sublimed from the cinquefoil. I'm not a shorts-and-shiver type, so I've taken off a layer of clothing and expect to remove another sweater shortly. Insect buzz becomes a background constant, bird song decreases in volume and frequency, thoughts of waiting chores vanish like the frost. The heat of a summer day pervades and reigns.

Boy, it's gonna be a hot one.

Old Dog, New Tricks
❦

Our second visit to Jackson Hole was in late summer, at a time so long ago few tourists remained after Labor Day. A few fishermen, fewer early hunters. It was so quiet that when we asked permission one afternoon to traverse a quarter-mile into the National Elk Refuge to look at trumpeter swans, we were readily granted it. No elk would be inconvenienced; they were still on their summer range, quite far away.

Meg and I proceeded merrily, looking at wildflowers, at rock formations, at sparrows and ravens and sky and mountains — somehow missing the approaching thunderstorm. We weren't thinking about rain, we weren't prepared for rain. This was pre-Gortex-this and lightweight-water-repellent-that. We had taken off our packs with our heavy war-surplus parkas and the like and left them behind. We were, after all, just going over *there* for a quick look.

We were happy and warm, enjoying a 70 degree summer day.

Within the limits of the thunderstorm, I can vouch, the temperatures fell to whatever is ambient on the dark side of the moon. The hail hurt. The rain was stunning in its ability to wet us down.

I've since thought about that wetting down, for we learned a lot about weather variability in the Rockies and about ourselves in those moments.

Not enough in that one lesson, though. Some years later, also on a late summer day, we went up Cascade Canyon in Grand Teton National Park on horseback. Nice warm day. We looked at wildflowers, at rock formations, at gray jays and ravens, at sky and mountains. We had one pack between us, one parka.

When the storm hit Meg was dry; she had on the parka and the one pair of gloves. I had a suede jacket and no gloves. To my uncertain recollection, it took a week to get back to the corral, to our motel, to a warm shower.

Have we now learned? We haven't duplicated those particular experiences, haven't been caught out hiking or on horseback with so little protection. But, there was a time recently when the raft went over and my non-waterproof pack contained imminently wettable matches and a change of wettable clothes. Enlightening.

An old dog needs to learn new tricks.

Visigoths
❧

Summer is winding down, Labor Day coming up. We decided to take a trip before snow to an archaeological site we'd read about for years, now protected as a state site. We enjoyed the petroglyphs and the ambience of their location: a little stream, small cliffs, rolling open country beyond. Pretty spot. Quiet. One could, almost, imagine a community of prehistoric people encamped here, gathering and hunting and having time for their ... art? Religion? Play? Making images.

We were encamped, also. Encumbered with 20th Century artifacts, yet serene.

And then the Visigoths arrived.

Hunters, dressed in paramilitary garb (camouflage, but with military caps, boots, and bandoleers), mounted on gasoline-powered, all-terrain steeds. Knives, lanterns. Racks of razor-tipped arrows, compound bows.

Summer

They were quiet once they'd settled in, considering the macho atmosphere, the many buggies, and the general feeling that a militia was preparing for Desert Storm, Part II.

We were settled in, too, reluctant to move on. And then, one grim-faced, full-rigged commando marched off to the toilet carrying, but trailing behind him, a huge roll of pink toilet paper. Pink. Toilet paper. Talk about a ruined image.

We smiled into our gin drinks. And slept soundly.

Fall

Touch of Fall
❧

A touch of fall today. Not yet Labor Day, but unmistakably fall. Hay in stacks. Willow and cottonwood leaves beginning to yellow; aspen leaves making a dry rustle. Last evening in Grand Teton National Park, we heard elk bugling. Already! Great Zeus.

Even insects are in on the act. Hummingbird moths are foraging in flower gardens and on the valley floor hummingbirds are now scarce: Only a diminishing number of females and young remain. Hairy caterpillars inch their way to important destinations. Porcupines scuttle about.

Touch of fall. Cool mornings, delicious days, frosty evenings. We parked north of Jackson near Flat Creek bridge for an hour or so one day recently. An autumn hatch of wonderfully interesting and rather large bugs swarmed over the creek. Cliff and barn swallows were after the bugs. So were cedar waxwings, but the swallows—especially the barn swallows—were spectacularly active. Their young had just fledged and were being fed on the wing.

One fledgling had made it to the top of a buckrail fence post overhanging the creek. And that was where he meant

to stay. He did not want to fly: He wanted to be back in his nest under the bridge.

After a bit we readily picked his parents out of the parade of other swallows. They never flew far from their baby, bringing him food in lightning-fast exchanges. Between each feeding, the little swallow simply hunkered

Fledgling

down on the fence, pretending he was someplace else. Two weeks old and out in the wild world—and hating it.

His parents were frustrated. They took food to their baby, but they really wanted him to fly. They coaxed him, hovering just out of reach, holding food out to tempt. They sat with him for a few moments, offering comfort and moral support. They slow-motioned their wings to demonstrate how easy flying actually is, and how much fun. They finally buffeted him with wing and bodies, trying to shove him into flight. No way. He stubbornly dug in and hung tough.

Later, in response to some unknown stimulus and without hesitation, the little swallow flew off, joining the flock skimming and circling over the creek. Indistinguishable. Fledged. Flying.

Had to learn to do it. Touch of fall in the air.

The Cusp
❦

It's September 8th ... maybe the 9th.

Trees are touched with yellow along the river.

The willows. The narrowleaf cottonwoods. Sweet clover in bloom. Knapweed, an undesirable weed that everyone wants to eradicate, is thriving. Seems to me "they" oughta come down here and wipe it out. I've pulled at it, whacked away at it, cursed at it. It's more tenacious than I. So is houndstooth, which I've had a tiny bit better luck with. Not much, though.

Little rain shower this morning. I don't think there was lightning. Maybe it will help put out a few fires ... that'd be nice. Being threatened by a forest fire rivets a guy's attention. A recent scare just west of us was, well, alerting.

Slightly fall-looking clouds. A little hatch of bugs ...

but I can't see a swallow anywhere. I'm sure there are still some in the valley. Yesterday, a bald eagle cruised down the river. Today, Canada geese are along the bank, as is a female common merganser. She's swimming actively, poking her bill rapidly in and out of the water. A yellow warbler, a few chickadees, a little family group of goldfinches fly by; they nest in late summer.

The sunshine is diluted this morning. I can't see the top of the Grand Teton ... it's obscured by clouds. Big swirling clouds: some white, some gray, some ominous, some puffy cumulus. Looking south, the Snake River Range stands out, sharply, defined by snow.

The day teeters, on the cusp between summer and fall. Delightful.

Memory Walk
❦

We used to walk to the Forks of Cascade Canyon in Grand Teton National Park. We walked park trails in September back when one met perhaps six people on an all-day hike. Or none.

Assuming the statute of limitations has run its course, I confess that we often took our puppy with us on seldom-used trails. Keep in mind that in those long-ago times, park rangers would direct people to archaeological sites and urge them to pick up arrowheads and other artifacts.

I'm pretty sure rangers don't do that anymore. They can rest assured, too, that we are scrupulous about where our puppy sets foot now. The last time we walked up Cascade Canyon we were puppyless; there were plenty of people, however. People taking great strides, appearing out of nowhere and disappearing in a scuff or two in some of the fanciest footwear I've ever seen— or ever hope to see. Making more impact than our dog could ever do...

No matter. We were deliberately taking our time, enjoying the whole experience of being outdoors, sweating in the bright September sun, cooling off in the shade, listening to everything: wind and water, bird and bug, our own breathing and footfall. Tuning out other hikers as best we could. Stopping for any excuse at all, just shambling along immersing ourselves in the day and place. Imagining the higher places, trying to make mental pictures of the views.

I don't expect to get to the Forks again, unless a battalion of friends organizes a trek with caches of foodstuffs, medicines and sleeping gear every half-mile. Or less. Stuff for, oh, a week.

Not much chance I'd permit that. Or that they'd do it. But a chance ...

Over the years we've come upon moose, elk, pine marten, dipper, harlequin duck, and red-tailed hawk. We've walked in snow and wind and once, on horseback, rode

through a memorable sleet and ice storm. Wildflowers—
the gamut. Scenery—well, y'know, it's the Grand Tetons.
Incomparable.

It adds up to an indefinable feeling of having spent some
hours wisely and well.

I've just taken a memory walk to the Forks. Thanks.

Private Concert

I heard the dipper sing this morning.

The full song, complete with repeated burbles, trills and
phrases, accentuated with characteristic *zeeet* notes.

The remarkable little bird was foraging in a run of shallow riffles newly exposed in a seasonally shallow Snake
River. It walked and hopped upstream, disappearing below and reappearing above the water with unstudied indifference. I noticed its beak open and close as it ate, but not
when it sang. It surely must ...? But I couldn't detect any
movement.

The dipper is, at first glance, not a striking bird. Rather
drab and dumpy. Sometimes it will stand quietly next to
partially exposed, wet stream cobble, resembling one more
stone—until it moves. It walks beneath the water's surface.
It bobs up-and-down, flicking its nictitating eyelid to ex-

pose a white eye ring.   It flies low, hugging the water in erratic, caroming zigzags from one stream bank to another.

The dipper's song is arresting; it certainly stops me on my trudges.   It's heard year-round, but is, perhaps, most welcome to a listener on a frigid February morning.

I didn't see another dipper to whom my singer was directing its aria; when it eventually flew off, it wasn't joined by a companion.

I assumed it sang just for me. Bravo.

Still Home
❦

I have observations — of various kinds and details, too many in memory only — of aspects of the natural history of Jackson Hole made over some period of time.   When I can ignore my aches and pains, I tend to think of it as hardly any time at all.

Wasn't it just yesterday that Meg and I and our first puppy, Nipper, came to Jackson Hole?

Well, no.

The first white man known or believed to have seen Jackson Hole was John Colter, in 1806-7. We didn't meet.

Occasional, small groups of explorers passed through the valley during the rest of the 19th century, including Ashley, Hoback, Reznor, McKenzie and Smith. Just prior to the 20th century, a few bachelor males and a handful of families settled year-round. Settlement came late, came slowly.

Survival was touch-and-go; isolation and the severe climate were deadly obstacles.

Thus, the history of the region, as whites measure it, has been short—perhaps a century, take away various treks by early explorers (and conveniently disregarding Native Americans).

Meg and I have memories of half that period of time. Holy cow. No wonder I ache.

Many of our memories are of September. We chose that month as our vacation time in the Hole. In our first years we experienced a sense of the glory of extensive, expansive wildflower bloom by hiking into the high meadows.

Oh, sure, we never saw spring beauty or elephant's head, but we reveled at vistas of other wondrous blooms.

September gave us summer days, fall days, first snows, and suggestions of forthcoming winters. I like to think we were learning about the fauna and flora of the region—except for Uinta ground squirrels. The chiselers of local terminology were in hibernation before we arrived. As a result, we missed the largest number of hawks, which leave when their prey burrows underground. We also missed quite a few nesting bird species that migrate by late August.

Of course, we never really missed 'em—we were too busy looking at everything else.

Fall

Jackson Hole used to shut down in the fall. Miles of river and lake front with no other fishermen. No rafts. No depth-finders. Not many professional guides. It wasn't hard to believe we were great fishermen, even when deep down we knew better.

The trails were uncrowded. We were allowed to walk on the National Elk Refuge, since no elk likely had migrated by September. We relaxed with locals, who were relaxing after a hectic four-month tourist season. We drank significant numbers of mixed drinks with impunity at the one open hotel in town. Famous then, notorious now, for selling mix with little alcoholic beverage.

Some things never change.

And some things are always in flux. Animal populations, for example. Short-term cycles are difficult to assess. Take this summer's end, in the mid-1990s. Ground squirrels, mice and voles are down in number, as are buteos, coyotes and badgers. Skunks are increasing; who would have expected that? The region is in a hot/dry period; as moist breeding areas disappear, insects and insect-eating birds are in turn reduced.

But there's no shortage of people, houses, cars, aircraft, river rafts, and bicycles.

I guess my observations are less limited to natural history than they were not so long ago: People have intruded to such a large extent.

Fall

Wildlife inevitably loses out to human habitation. Civility loses out, too. I believe once a town's population exceeds 3,500, much is lost. One doesn't know everyone else, his favorite fishing hole or hunting stand is "discovered," parking becomes tougher. The night sky is obliterated by lights. Well, you know.

And yet. And yet. Summer is over. A certain calm settles, if only for a while. People have time to acknowledge your greeting; a few potluck dinners bring folks together.

It's not the same, but it's home.

Musical Companion
❦

On a recent walk I was being helped along by a brisk, sometimes pushy wind, when I heard music: a vaguely atonal, but not unpleasant snatch of unfamiliar song, coming from nowhere I could make out.

There was no one around except for the puppy and me. To be certain, I looked in the understory of the cottonwoods for Pan or, maybe, Kokopelli.

Nothing. No one.

What in the world? Then, it dawned on me: It was coming from my new cane, my all new high-tech, high performance, ultra-light, whiz-bang cane, made from aluminum tubing. Its length is adjusted by a spring-loaded doo-dad which propels what looks like a ball bearing into a selected hole among a succession of punched holes spaced an inch apart along its axis. Surely you've seen the device. No? Well, anyway, the holes were not so intended, but when the wind is blowing at least 30 mph and coming from the correct quarter, the cane becomes a flute of sorts: a hollow pipe with air rushing through the holes. Ancient design.

The optimal direction for the wind is from my right hind quarter. I've experimented, and that's it. If the air is still, I can twirl the cane and, sometimes, make music.

I'm easily amused.

I've accepted the cane, even though that acceptance was psychologically difficult and the cane itself is too high-tech for me. It appeared one day via a decision made by a strong-willed friend. It's lightweight but strong. Anodized. Brownish orange. I'm content with that color; I wouldn't like black or shiny silver. It has a padded handle, a rubber tip for ordinary use, and an optional cleated ice prong that folds up when not needed — but still manages to snag pants cuffs and automobile upholstery.

My cane has a wrist-strap on its handle. It's light enough that I can easily lift it and ignore its presence when I raise my binoculars to look at something. A handy feature.

So, I have a new companion on my strolls now.

Whoopee.

Fall

Equinox
❦

Morning of the autumnal equinox. Down by the river-side, two adult bald eagles sit side-by-side on a tree limb they use as a hunting perch. I'm surprised to see adult eagles together in September. They must have escaped their young for the first time in half a year and gone off by themselves ... a romantic rendezvous.

No, I don't really think that.

They just seem relaxed and companionable.

Within my binocular view of the eagles runs the fabled Snake River, a low fog bank, a stretch of yellowing cotton-woods and, in the foreground, a belted kingfisher perches on the root of a grounded tree snag. Easy on the eye, on the psyche.

At autumnal equinox, daylight hours approximate the daylight available in spring. Many bird species respond with renewed mating and nesting urges. It's easier to notice this tendency in larger birds. Those eagles? Perhaps. An osprey or hawk may take a branch or two to refurbish the old home-stead. Grouse not infrequently strut. A songbird may surprise with a burst of song. And ravens—ah, ravens are pretty much full-time lovers.

Fall

Simultaneously, a few territorial defense mechanism hormones fire up: Birds that have sailed across the home base of other species unchallenged for weeks are surprised to be chased away. Bald eagles and osprey spar without a fish involved. Here and there, a red-winged or Brewer's blackbird will chase a raven briefly.

The correct term to describe this activity is phenological response. Phenology studies relationships between climate and periodic phenomena, as in bird migration and nesting, or flowering of plants. These related phenomena are often ephemeral, but enjoyable to find.

In a few weeks I hope to see and remark upon "late" flowering harebells, lupine, scarlet gilia, and other wildflowers. Happens late every fall, and always a pleasure to see.

A special day. Brings to mind the mating urge. Think I'll gather up Meg and take her out to lunch.

All the World's A Stage
❦

This morning I watched a male Brewer's blackbird chase a spotted sandpiper until the sandpiper had to take refuge in, and beneath, the Snake River. The blackbird then took after a killdeer, attacking it and hazing it for a good 100 yards before the killdeer hung a left and vamoosed. Such a nice morning. Such an early morning grouch. Wonder what pulled his chain?

Maybe he was kicked out (with good reason) from one of the blackbird flocks. With winter approaching, birds everywhere are staging for migration, gathering in tight-knit communities. Flocks of waterfowl, swirling mobs of swallows, ground-hugging platoons of sparrows and juncoes, trees-full of warblers and flycatchers. Nesting competition is over; tolerance of others is accepted, even welcomed.

Staging, a preparation for migration, is Nature's way of getting an individual bird to feel comfortable in company of its kind, a time to build up fat resources and energy for the hazards and effort of migration ahead. A time of waiting for that moment when everything is right: daylight hours, food supplies, internal clocks and internal restlessness, wind direction and barometer. And then, to go.

By September, some bird species — including warblers, sparrows, flycatchers and male hummingbirds — are long gone. Other species hang on for months. A few come out of the mountains to the valley floor and call that a migration. Some simply stay where they are all year.

Seems birds are just like people.

And it's not just the birds. Elk assemble in small groups, called harems, in preparation for mating. Migration comes later. Deer begin to herd. Antelope bunch together. Cows bring themselves down out of the high country.

Fall

I don't have a good word for the cattle's behavior. Overdomestication, perhaps.

If I were a bird, I'd like staging. Hang out together, eat and get fat, and then go South.

I guess that Brewer's blackbird just had a tough night.

Mothering Up

Ranchers moved their cattle down from the mountains, the summer range, this week. Not a drive, exactly, for the cattle had recognized the onset of fall and begun to drift down weeks ago on their own hook. Cows don't appear to be too bright — somewhere on the lower end of the intelligence bell curve — but they need ranch hands to keep vehicles from running into them on the roads.

There's a lot of confusion when hundreds of cows move tens of miles on a given morning. Calves get separated from their mothers who bellow for their babies. When a layover or the ultimate destination is reached, the herd mills around, cows bellowing, calves bleating, in attempts to find each other. The process is called "mothering up."

The back-and-forth bellowing, mooing, bleating, and restlessness continues for days. Anxiety, confusion and tension fill the air. We love it, even though the critters obviously don't.

145

Moreover, it works. Ultimately, each mother finds her baby. Non-stop mooing ceases. The herd settles down into a routine, the atmosphere of excitement slowly abates.

Not quite-so-dumb cows.

Autumn Color
❦

A September morning in a high mountain valley in the Rockies. Twenty-six degrees, no wind, quiet. Quiet. No raven call, no chickadee notes. Even the river seems to run smoothly, oleaoginously. The water reflects the gold and yellows, the very occasional reds of narrowleaf cottonwoods and their associated understory shrubs of the riparian zone.

Silently, one by one, a leaf here, a leaf there, gives up and twirls to earth. So many leaves that in an hour's time there is no detectable change in the scene, but if a particular tree or shrub is studied even for a quarter hour, its branches and trunk begin to emerge as distinct shapes.

I walk to a group of trees and allow myself to be suffused in color. Autumn color in every direction, beneath my feet, above my head. I am acutely aware that this particular color wheel is transitory; leaves are constantly in the air, obeying gravity's summons.

A hint that winter is not far behind.

Passing Through

White-crowned sparrows were "passing through" Jackson Hole as September came to an end, scouring shrubs and underbrush around lakeshores and along stream edges. They moved south in loose, small flocks, keeping in touch with one another with soft notes. Little inconspicuous birds, each on a monumental journey.

A hundred other bird species "pass through" Jackson Hole twice a year on migration. For some reason, white-crowned sparrows pass through all over the country. Meg has chuckled over this specialization of the white-crowned sparrow, wondering mildly where all the young white-crowns come from if the birds are always on the wing. Good point. This morning I notice the white-crowns dominate the bird scene. Robins, blackbirds, flycatchers, tanagers, and shorebirds have all scrammed.

What a pity. A bird watcher must content himself with gold and brown and russets in tree and shrub, with varying brilliant yellows and a few reds in aspens, the wine of geranium leaves, the astonishing still-bright-green of a willow or chokecherry, a last-of-the-season harebell or aster, with a golden expanse of sagebrush and the deep green of evergreen forests. With the mountains, the rivers, the sky and clouds. This bird watcher feels no sense of deprivation. None whatsoever.

That Lovin' Feeling
❦

This October day we decided to drive into the Gros Ventre Mountains to look around and, with luck, spot some bighorn sheep — always a psychological boost. We were surprised by a pair of moose along the Gros Ventre River, across from the National Elk Refuge. They were in a meadow opening among tall cottonwood trees; we had come upon their tryst.

Well, maybe not a "tryst." Watching the activity, I didn't get the impression the male was as pleased to be there as the female. (Kids these days.) She was putting moves on this guy one ordinarily sees only in R-rated movies. Or, X-rated. She followed him around, headed him off, showed him her best end, made endearing moans and sighs: A lascivious hussy.

It was doggone educational.

The prime student was a yearling female calf, which stayed far enough away to not get trampled but close enough to get an earful and an eyeful.

Fall

The about-to-pair pair soon wandered out of sight, closely attended by the calf. I wanted to witness consummation, but following them would've been folly beyond understanding. I've absolutely no doubt mating occurred that pleasant afternoon. Trust me on this.

We went into the mountains and saw sheep, and trumpeter swans, and ripe rose hips, and red hills, and green water and blue skies. All very wonderful, indeed — but the moose tableaux overshadowed everything else and remains the uppermost memory of that day.

A 90-year-old man, upon noticing a voluptuous young woman at a party, is said to have remarked, "I wish I were 80 again."

I know how he felt.

Moose cow and calf

Fall

Storm Approach
❦

An early morning fog is lifting as I begin my walk, with the puppy as an excuse. As the fog dissipates, I become aware of songbird movement. They're flying in little flocks — waves actually — through the bare understory, the spruce and aspen. There's urgency in their passage, a scurrying search for nourishment, a disinclination to preen or sing or even call. They know a storm is coming. Cirrus clouds finger the sky.

It should come as no surprise that animals sense the approach of a storm. Heck, if I can — not entirely civilized but far from wild — certainly a smart animal can. It's flattering and self-aggrandizing for humans haughtily to assume they're the smartest animal in the hierarchy.

The little bands of chickadees, white-crowned sparrows, kinglets and yellow-rumped warblers move south along the river, following the bird-and-ungulate migration corridor through Jackson Hole's steppe. They fly from tree to tree, shrub to perhaps fence post or mullein, rock to still flowering lupine. It suggests aimlessness but in moments they're gone. A lone robin and cedar waxwings hurtle past.

Fall

The clouds have already begun to broaden, congregating, veiling the sun. A breeze comes from wherever winds are stored, stirring the leaves and bending branches.

Safe journey, little feathered friends. Hurry on.

Gravity
🍂

The cottonwoods have changed overnight. Over one night, or so I firmly believe, the trees have become leafless mandrels, skeletons, bare shapes; this morning they look gray. I stare, unwilling to accept the evidence before me and bewildered at what I think to be such suddenness. But finally I accept it: Summer is gone.

Not just over: Gone. It's a week-and-a-half into October. I can only hope for a spell of Indian summer, that splen-

Aspen leaf

151

did, if only occasional, period of days or weeks that follows the first frosts of fall. The last chance to do outdoor chores before winter arrives, the last chance to hike or drive to some special place before it's covered by snow. To get winter clothing washed or cleaned. To get firewood. To get psyched for winter.

Years ago we got psyched up for winter. Now we just get psyched for winter.

A good friend's professor often stated that, "eventually one must accede to the blandishments of gravity." That is a truism, I guarantee. We still enjoy winter, but we don't play with it the way we once did.

I stand on a little rise above the river, and try for a while to paste the leaves back on the trees in my imagination. I try to see last week's colors, but with little success: My imagination isn't up to the task. It's over.

Gravity's blandishments have won.

Balloon Spiders
☙

A peachy Indian summer day.

A crisp morning, a sparkling sky, a sure promise of a warm, languid afternoon.

Fall

A sense of well-being. On top of that, a wonderful fore-knowledge that all those chores around the house I really did mean to complete will soon be covered by snow and out of sight. Too nice today to fuss with details; there may be no more enjoyable pre-winter days this year.

And this day balloon spiders have chosen to migrate.

Balloon spiders climb up on something high—a fence post or tree perhaps—spin out a long filament of "silk" and on a day such as this, when balmy afternoon thermals and zephyrs arise, allow themselves to be carried away on gossamer wings.

They're quite literally up in the air, subject to whatever befalls them. When the breeze dies they come to earth wherever they happen to be. Their discarded threads are found suspended in trees, on fences, festooning patches of range or ranch, on cars and ponds. In late afternoon and early mornings, slanting rays of sun define loops and cantilevers of silk, revealing the landing zone of an individual spider.

Indian summer days and humid summer mornings—when dew outlines their webs—are about the only times balloon spiders become obvious. They're small, possessing only 1/20-inch long bodies and moderately sized legs. They live quietly, in ground litter and on grasses. They live so quietly they've escaped widespread scientific notice: I've yet to find much about their lives. This is their day in the sun, so to speak—their 15 minutes of fame.

Fall

I'm really not fond of insects and their allies. But I'd rather stand and applaud these little voyageurs than do my chores.

Too nice a day to do anything mundane.

Raynes Site 1

❦

Except for a few petroglyphs at the head of the Gros Ventre River, just barely within the topographical limits of Jackson Hole, there are no examples of ancient people's rock art in the valley. That is the accepted view, certainly, and try as we have to find any more, Meg and I haven't done so.

Maybe the rock is too hard — or too soft. Maybe, as migrating hunter/gatherers, they didn't have the time (I very much doubt this idea.) Maybe some remain to be found. Certainly there is rock art not far from Jackson Hole — and we've found artifacts and seen collections of various implements, tools, decorative items here. Firm evidence of paleo-Indians has been found all over the valley, but somewhat mysteriously art has been excluded.

So, we always look for it.

One lovely fall day we were wandering around in the Gros Ventre Mountains, following a little drainage looking for — whatever would come.

Fall

It was late in the season. We saw few flowers, but considerable sign of deer and elk. At one point Meg was scrutinizing a south-facing hillside, dry enough to support some of the few juniper trees in Jackson Hole.

Her attention was drawn to something ... something involving a juniper tree that just didn't seem natural. Something too regular, something out-of-place. She doesn't remember precisely what triggered the ensuing tingle of recognition, of excitement, but it became a "something" that required closer examination.

It was a small cave, large enough for one person hunting, perhaps two at most. Its opening was slightly augmented with a wall of local stone that incorporated the juniper's trunk. From it, one could view a forested slope leading to a small stream.

If an elk or deer were to emerge, it would be in clear unobstructed sight. Some distance away, true, but downhill from the cave and within range of arrow or spear.

We made a careful visual examination, not disturbing anything, and found no white man's artifacts. No match or pop-top or cigarette butt or cartridge shell. No plastic. Several years later when the cave was examined by the Wyoming state archaeologist (there are many sites and not enough archaeologists), nothing related to man was found.

We assumed immediately it was a hunting blind, although some thought was given to the possibility it was a

155

vision quest location. We doubt that. Professional archaeologists believe it could be as much as 500 years old: lichen
covers part of the rock wall and tree trunk. We think it
younger, but we simply don't know. Nobody yet knows.

While not an important find, the cave is officially on
the archaeological register as Raynes Site 1, which tickles
us.

We're still looking for Raynes Site II.

Hunting
🍂

What seems like a long time ago, we hunted, Meg and
I. For the meat, for the challenge of trying to get close to
game, for an autumn outing, for the companionship. For a
while we rather enjoyed it, especially when we were able to
range substantial distances — and particularly at sunrise
when the autumn sun illumines the Tetons in a reveal which
catches the breath no matter how often one is privileged to
view it.

We stopped hunting when we couldn't get into the
backcountry any longer. We soon discovered we were sur-
rounded by shooters, not hunters — shooters of the kind who
once pinned us down behind fallen aspen trees and blasted
19 shots in our direction. I guess they never heard us yell-

ing, or they thought elk could yell. Or didn't really care what they shot at, so long as they got to shoot.

I won't pretend we were great white hunters. I was often reminded by companions that if I kept watching birds, I was going to miss seeing the hoofed creatures. But we weren't shooters, and didn't enjoy their company. Thus, we don't hunt the wily wapiti any more.

On some October and November mornings now, in the pre-dawn expectation of cloudless sky and movement of elk from meadows to deep woods, there's a certain urge in me — surpressed only by a third cup of coffee in a warm kitchen.

Crane Fly
❦

One evening in late October. My attention is drawn to a lone crane fly on top of quiet backwater on the Snake River. It's zipping across the surface so quickly it's leaving a wake — creating a bow wave, of all things.

Crane flies are big, floppy insects that resemble over-sized mosquitoes. These giants don't seem to bite humans. Fortunately. They often swarm near incandescent lamps. They're known to fly slowly and walk more slowly. Admirable traits.

Not this one. It wasn't being pursued, it wasn't trapped; it was apparently simply feeding on algae ... algae that wasn't going anywhere fast. Yet it flew at flank speed from cobble to stick, stick to algae patch, algae patch to open water for at least 10 minutes after I happened by.

One crane fly doing something out of custom.

Perhaps someone knows why. I've never noticed this before, but I don't study insects carefully. Maybe crane flies do aerobics all the time, and this guy was just out for an evening jog. Gee. I know people who do that ... and I don't understand why they do it either.

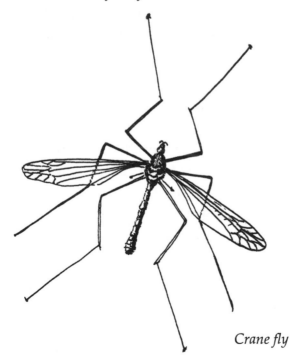

Crane fly

Cranky

Nothing in Nature is ever quite the same year to year. There's winter, sure, and spring, summer and fall; there's cold and hot; drought and "too much" rain. But, within those often vague distinctions lies a wondrous variability. Wondrous and entrancing.

The past dozen years or so have featured relatively benign winters. There've been only a few weeks of truly attention-getting, brutal temperatures of minus 40, relatively few days of blocked roads, of hoofed animals desperate to gain access to grasses or browse. Relatively few weeks on end of rain and gloom.

There's been too much drought in the 1980s and 1990s — certainly — and higher temperatures the last decade. And lots more wind. Old-timers never mentioned so much wind; they surely would've talked about it if it'd been a large fact of life.

On the whole, North America has been enjoying — no, that implies recognition — North America has been truly blessed by a weather bonanza for a half century. We should

159

be more grateful and more attentive to climatic cycles — particularly the potential of global warming.

I notice that prolonged periods of cold or heat or rain get people grumpy. Oh, not you? I bet. Monotony seems to dull everybody's psyche. Does mine. I can develop cabin fever during any month of the year. Actually, it's most virulent for me during mud season. When snow melt makes dirt roads impassable and paved streets uncomfortable and over-snow travel miserable, I develop a tad bit of crankiness. Or so I've been told. And I believe it. Variety jazzes things up, including nature study.

Birds, in particular, seem to get stuck in a monotonous pattern of lowered activity during prolonged barometric stability — high, low, or in-between.

This isn't a complaint. Long ago, I figured out I can't control the weather by hoping for this or that kind of day; I just try to take each day as it comes.

Don't ask me to prove that if it's been raining for three solid weeks, or minus 35 degrees, or (worse yet) 90 plus. I can, indeed, develop a tad of crankiness.

First Snow
❦

Well, here it is: the expected unexpected. The first real snow. Oh, there've been flurries, skiffs, dustings, and sure, there's snow on the peaks and in the canyons, behind rocks, and within forests — but this one fell in the valley. It sits on the grasses and roofs, in the driveways and on the fences. The first snow.

It came announced by the wind.

I like to think of this valley as having relatively little wind, yet in recent years we've had more and more windy days, and higher and higher velocity winds. Yesterday was a doozy. Sometime shortly after midnight the wind swooshed into the Hole and blew for 18 hours. It blew at treetop level; it blew at ground level. All day long layered clouds streamed past at different levels and varying speeds.

When the wind stopped — twice — around 9 o'clock last night, the silence was eerie. And then, of course, came the snow, falling straight down through silent darkness. Large, slow flakes quickly covered the ground, buried leaf litter, clung to evergreen needles, defined the trails, outlined the river banks.

And, on this sunny morning, snow blankets the whole scene.

A nice scene. The Snake River, at its winter-low flow, has bare rock riffles where a dipper vigorously plies its trade. Bordering the river are the bare trunks and freshly wind-pruned branches of cottonwoods and willow, of snowberry and sage, against a darker background of spruce. To my northwest, the Tetons are snow-covered down to 7,000 feet, less than a thousand feet above me. The sky directly above is light blue, but to the south dark-bottomed, threatening clouds suggest another flurry may come. Exposed river cobbles are white with snow. A few glisten wetly as they warm in response to the sun's first rays.

There will be an adjustment, a selective loss of snow cover this day. Some will vanish from my and the puppy's tracks, some from metal posts, some from branches, some from south-facing, windswept ridges and slopes. Much will remain for the duration of winter — five, perhaps six, months.

I rather welcome this snow. I'm glad it's not a huge fall because I haven't finished my outdoor chores, and may yet get a chance.

On the other hand, I'd welcome not having to finish them.

It's probably a good thing choices in the natural world are made for us. So far anyway.

Winter on the Wing

Cold, but not yet severely cold. No wind, so the temperatures are tolerable. One can deal with cold alone, but wind plus cold becomes threatening in an instant. A light

ground fog burnt off early this morning. Some of the moisture refroze into large diamond-shaped flakes which fell in
a cheerful slow motion to cluster on limb and branch, and
freshened the week-old snow. Sparkly glitters, reflecting a
dim sunshine. A kind of crystalline forest and field.

Admiring the frost for as long as it lasts, I am slow to
recognize that the river has far more waterfowl — goldeneyes,
mergansers, and even mallards — than it has harbored for a
couple of months. I've been expecting this to happen; when
Yellowstone Lake freezes over and creeks ice up, waterfowl
move onto the larger rivers or to places where open water is
maintained (as by thermal activity).

These birds are still unaccustomed to their new surrounding. They're restless, forming and re-forming little
bunches. Not feeding, but investigative. Some will now
remain in the Hole for the duration of winter, some will move
south. Much depends on the severity of this particular winter, but unless the Snake River freezes entirely over — wow!
that must be something to witness — some will remain until
mid spring.

The ice crystals have gone. Sublimed. Leaving no dis-
cernible trace. The sky has changed. Ice has appeared in it.
Cirrus clouds sweep in a broad band from the southwest,
overtaking the sun, chilling me and the world around it. It's
going to snow. Not predicted, but it's going to snow. A
little wind comes along, suggesting I pull down earflaps and

put on gloves. I change my route; I like to walk home with wind at my back when the wind is chill.

Snow Geese
❦

It's gray with alternate rain and snow showers, precipitation that melts some of the four inches of snow cover rather than adding to it. It's a raw, rather unpleasant morning.

Fog and clouds hover just above the valley floor: The Tetons don't exist except for an occasional glimpse of their base.

It's a snow goose day ... the kind of day that magnificent bird migrates through Jackson Hole. I don't know why — I don't think anyone does — but the snow geese must. They tend to fly in flocks close to the Tetons steep, east-facing slopes, following the Snake River at the mountain/steppe interface. Most birds use this corridor in migration, but avoid flying in fog and rain and clouds. Not snow geese.

So, I'm not surprised to get a telephone call from an observer who has just spotted a dozen snow geese, the first he's seen in this region. Their occurrence is irregular; sometimes several years pass between sightings.

I dash out and look and listen. No luck. But I'm saddled up and my boots are already wet, so what the heck: I whistle up the puppy and go out along the river, listening high.

Fall

Welcoming Winter
🍎

Some locals, especially as they get older, "go out" for winter if they can. They go to places warmer than the Hole in winter: Arizona, California, southern Utah. To Dubois, Wyoming, even.

We don't.

We probably could—we even did a couple of winters for health reasons—but we don't. Why not? Put simply, Jackson Hole is beautiful in winter.

The Hole slips into the cold season starting just after Labor Day when the peak of tourist hustle passes.

Locals are weary. Many go to the deserts of Wyoming ostensibly to hunt sage grouse—or "chicken hunt"— and they do kill some. Mostly it's an unwinding, a chance to greet friends and catch up on whatever may have happened to them over the summer. To relax and party and talk. Old-timers who stay in the valley have potluck gatherings.

Aspens turn to gold and orange, cottonwoods to yellow, mountain maples bedeck the Snake River Canyon red. Mountain tops are dusted then covered with snow, snow that spills down the canyons and slopes into the forests. In the valley, the snow is rain— rain that washes clean the dust of summer, every tree and remaining leaf, shrub and rock.

Fall

The sky in late October also seems washed clean; from the valley floor the spectacular colors of gneiss, feldspar, quartz, granite and limestone — rocks that comprise the bare tops of the Tetons — are unnaturally brilliant.

Streams and rivers are perfectly clear. Fishing is good, wildlife re-emerges and is seen more frequently.

"Think Snow" bumper stickers appear. Our old friend Bob begins to rub his lucky belt buckle which reads SNOW, which he believes brings the snows that close many dirt and little-used roads for the season. It makes us feel snug rather than isolated.

We don't shun winter; we welcome it. Reserving the right to grumble, of course. A right granted to everyone who has spent at least 20 winters in Jackson Hole.

And, dammit, to no one else.

Full Circle

Solstice

❦

W inter solstice, once more.   Today the sun "stands
still" — an instant calculated these days not just to
the day and hour, but to the minute and second.
Earth moves around the sun in an elliptical orbit while re-
volving on an inclined axis, as a result daylight periodically
diminishes, achieves this annual minimum and once more
increases. A year is thereby defined.

In the Northern Hemisphere this annual event occurs
around the third week of what we call December. On this
very day. The sun's return is of such consequence it's no
wonder mankind has marked the event by various means
for millennia. People who lived one hundred and fifty generations ago built stone houses with purposeful apertures

aligned to solstices, carved stone symbols to capture ephemeral (but reproducible) indications of the sun's passage. They laid out astronomically accurate circles upon the ground.

For these peoples, as for us today, the days and weeks following the winter solstice have been times for celebration, for ritual, for expressions of faith. For the carrying of torches and the lighting of houses, to modern Hanukkah and Christmas celebrations. For expressions of faith and of gratitude that the sun will, indeed, return.

For weeks now days and nights have been superficially alike. The sun has set at nearly the same minute. Sunrise has gotten later and later, but by only a few minutes, so daylight hours have remained identical. Although I'm confident in the astronomers, I, too, need something to renew my faith. To reset my inner clock.

Nothing today.

A few days later: At our feeder, appearing for the first time in weeks, a band of chickadees, eating sunflower seeds, investigating aspen trees, being busy, being purposeful. They don't sing, but they seem especially merry. And in that instant, I know, I just know, that in a week or so, from some tree or shrub, on some calm winter day, a chickadee will respond to certain knowledge that the daylight hours have commenced to lengthen, even if just barely, and will sing. Tenuously, tentatively, perhaps a practice call. Enough to reassure me, to renew my faith that another year of wonderful happenings in the natural world has begun. Days will lengthen, other birds will sing, trees will bud, grass will grow, hibernating animals will wake, the earth will be renewed.

The summer solstice will come, too; and winter again. Full circle.

Notes

Academy Award Night
❦

On May 4, 1995, Bert and Meg Raynes were honored at a testimonial dinner by hundreds of friends and colleagues for their contributions to wildlife and the community of Jackson Hole. The gala event was held at the National Museum of Wildlife Art, an appropriate selection for a couple whose avocation for two decades has been wise stewardship of the valley's wildlife.

Representatives from the Wyoming Game and Fish Department, Grand Teton National Park, the National Elk Refuge, Teton Science School, the *Jackson Hole News*, and friends praised Bert and Meg for their unstinting efforts. Perhaps the most touching tributes were the announcements that a grove of cottonwood trees would be planted on the National Elk Refuge in Meg's honor, and a trail in Bert's name would be created on the National Elk Refuge near the Wyoming Travel Information Center on U.S. Hwy. 189.

Bert's thank you talk reflected the nature of the man being honored. Excerpts are printed below:

"I'm glad I had some advance warning about this evening. Even with it, we're pretty much overwhelmed..."

"I'd had one alert, but it didn't truly register: OK. A dinner. I like to eat. Then Meg came back one day after Ladies Lunch and remarked, 'You know, they are going to give you a *big* dinner .' My instant response was, 'I've got to update my will.' I figured this was going to be a memorial...

"As an old friend and colleague would state in times of stress and emotion, I am 'non-pulsed.'"

"We're very grateful to the many people directly involved in this event. I'm also in debt to—now I'm going to slip into my academy ward mode—to the *legions* of highly trained and dedicated physicians, surgeons, orthopedic surgeons, orthopods, neurologists, nurses, nurses' aides, volunteers, therapists, respiratory therapists, technicians, physical therapists, social workers, psychiatrists, psychologists ... whose heroic efforts have made it possible for me to be here tonight.

"And to look so *good*. A fine figure of a Victorian endomorphic gentleman.

"I have to thank the wildlife, including birds and not excluding alpha female cocker spaniels. Most particularly, most especially, I thank Meg Raynes. She truly deserves any recognition appropriate to this occasion. To any occasion. If I hadn't been so lucky as to meet her, I'm convinced I would never have learned to appreciate what it is I do appreciate about the natural world. Or for that matter, a great many other wonders. I'd likely have ended up in some big industrialized situation as a nerd-engineer type. Instead of as a nerd bird-watcher. Thanks, honey.

"Now then: A few words to this audience. I'm acutely aware that this audience is composed entirely of notable individuals who have accomplished far more, created far more, have been and are today — and will be tomorrow — more productive than I have ever been or will be. (I may have gotten away with more than any of you have, is all.)

"Each of you deserves, if you haven't already had it, a testimonial dinner of your own. And we'll come, won't we honey?

"But for tonight, and for as long as I can — a few days at least — I plan to pretend that I deserve even a portion of all of this. All these nice things you have all expressed. It just feels so good.

"When we came to Jackson Hole to stay, Meg and I were determined to try to fit into the community; looking around tonight, I entertain the notion that we didn't do too badly ... We also wanted to contribute to the community. You all seem to think we did reasonably OK in that desire, too. I'm not so generous in my evaluation, but tonight I'll accept yours.

"It's an inexpressible pleasure to think that a grove of cottonwood trees will flourish on the National Elk Refuge — within sight of this fine museum — where there might not otherwise be one. It gives me as much pleasure, anticipated delight, to have a nature boardwalk where people can stand or sit and observe wild things doing the things wild things do, and perhaps learn from those animals, birds, fish....

"In The Tragedy of Hamlet, Prince of Denmark — Act I, Scene III, Shakespeare has Polonius give sound, notable, quotable advice to his son, Laertes. Laertes is going off to France to school. Directions such as, 'This above all, to thine own self be true,' and 'It must follow as the night to day thou canst not be false to any man.' And, 'Give thy thoughts no tongue, nor any unproportion'd thought his act.'

"And, 'Thou friends thou hast and their adoption tried, grapple them to thy soul with hoops of steel ... '

"Friends, each of you is grappled to my soul."

Titles Not Chosen

❦

Memoirs of a Former Walking Person	Rambling With Bert
	Meandering With Bert
Walking in Beauty	Shuffling with Bert
Walks in Beauty	Marking Time
He Walks in Beauty	Not Far From the Car
Near Afield	Easy Walker
Barely Afield	Signs and Sentiments
Barely Afloat	Mountain Musings
Barely Alive	Mountain Moods
You Can Observe A Lot By Just Watching	Circling Home
	Signs of the Season
Downhill All the Way	Sometimes Finding the Signs
Woof Walks	

Production
❧

Rebecca Woods Bloom illustrated, photographed and designed *Valley So Sweet*. David Swift scanned the line drawings and photographs. The cover and manuscript of this book were prepared and submitted to Patterson Printing in Benton Harbor, Michigan, in electronic form. Text files were processed using Microsoft Word 5.1 and Aldus Pagemaker® 5.0.